THE Ancient World

John Doogan
Series editor: Jim McGonigle

Heinemann

Heinemann is an imprint of Pearson Education Limited, a company incorporated in England and Wales, having its registered office at Edinburgh Gate, Harlow, Essex, CM20 2JE. Registered company number: 872828

Heinemann is the registered trademark of Pearson Education Limited

© John Doogan 2002

First published 2002

ISBN 978 0 435 320911
09
10 9 8 7 6 5 4

Designed and typeset by Ken Vail Graphic Design

Illustrated by Peter Bull, Steve Smith and Ross Watton

Original illustrations © Heinemann Educational Publishers 2002

Printed and bound in the United Kingdom by Scotprint

Picture research by Charlotte Lipman

Photographic acknowledgements
The author and publishers would like to thank the following for permission to reproduce photographs: Corbis/Angel Hornak: 33B; Corbis/Bettmann: 41D; Corbis/Cordaiy Photo Library: 63B; Corbis/Eye Ubiquitous: 63A; Mary Evans Picture Library: 47B; Michael Holford: 10A, 16A, 19A, 19B, 21B, 22A, 22B, 24A, 27A, 28B, 48B, 54A, 55B, 57A; Mick Sharp: 6A; Middle East Pictures: 12A; Ronald Grant Archive/Deamworks/ Universal Pictures: 58B; Scotland in Focus: 37A, 41C; The Bridgeman Art Library/Egyptian National Museum, Cairo: 25D; Travel Ink/Andrew D.R. Brown: 34C; Travel Ink/Robin McKelvie: 7B; Werner Forman/Archive/British Museum: 40A; Werner Forman/Archive/National Museum of Ireland: 40B

Cover photograph © AKG/Jurgen Sorges

Written sources acknowledgements
The author and publishers gratefully acknowledge the following publications from which written sources in the book are drawn. In some sources the wording or sentence has been simplified.
F. Delaney, *The Celts* (Hodder and Stoughton, 1986): 41E
R. Rudgeley, *Secrets of the Stone Age* (Century, 2000): 4A
J. Simkin, *The Roman Empire* (Spartacus Educational, 1991): 59D

Contents

The origins of Stone Age people

The term 'prehistory' (see Source A) is used to describe the period before people could write down what happened in their lives.

Finding out about Stone Age people

Archaeological evidence includes many everyday objects used by early people, like tools, weapons, clothes, jewellery, and even chariots or carts. This evidence helps us to build up a picture of what life was like for the earliest peoples.

Archaeologists have also discovered the fossilised remains of human bodies buried thousands of years ago. Careful study of these human remains can tell us how they lived, what they ate and even what they looked like. Cave paintings and rock carvings also provide evidence of the life and appearance of early people.

If you just look at the history of an area of the world (such as Scotland or Egypt or Europe) and ignore the prehistoric background, then you get a very distorted and misleading picture. Prehistory makes up at least 95 per cent of the human story and history a mere 5 per cent. How can you ignore evidence from prehistory and still expect to make sense of our past?

Richard Rudgeley in Secrets of the Stone Age.

Finding food and shelter in the Stone Age

As early people developed they made tools and weapons from stone and this period is therefore known as the Stone Age. Life for Stone Age people must have been very hard. They ate nuts and berries and hunted small animals. For shelter they lived in caves. The discovery of fire was very important as it allowed them to keep warm, cook food and frighten away wild animals. The skins of animals were sewn together, using bone needles, to make clothes.

Timeline of the Evolution of Humans

c. 4 million years ago The first human-apes or hominids appear in Africa. (Their fossilised remains have been found in Tanzania in eastern Africa.) It is believed that they originally live in trees, but evolve and begin to walk on the ground on two legs.

c. 2 million years ago The first true humans appear: *Homo habilis*. The first 'upright human', *Homo erectus*, appears about 300,000 years later.

c. 200,000 years ago Wise humans, or *Homo sapiens*, begin to flourish. Homo sapiens are much more like people today.

The first farmers

In the Old Stone Age (also called the **Palaeolithic** age) man was a hunter. After the Ice Age the first farmers began to appear, around 8000 BC. People began to tame some wild animals: herding animals had many advantages over hunting and killing them. At the same time early people learned how to **cultivate** (grow) crops such as wheat and barley: this allowed people to settle in one place.

A Stone Age family in their cave.

Tools and weapons

The earliest people made tools and weapons from stone. Gradually they discovered that a particular type of stone – flint – was especially good for this purpose. The first weapons made in the Old Stone Age were hand-axes. As they became more skilful early people made knives, chisels and engraving tools.

Early peoples developed at different rates in different parts of the world; the first farmers were cultivating crops in the Middle East around 8000 BC, but the first farming in Scotland only started around 4000 years later. Many modern writers have presented an image of prehistoric people as barbaric or uncivilised. However, monuments built by early peoples, such as Stonehenge in England, the Standing Stones at Callinish on the Isle of Lewis in Scotland or the prehistoric temples of Malta and Gozo suggest that even before the rise of the culture of Ancient Egypt, early peoples had achieved high levels of knowledge and lived in organised communities.

Questions

1. List the different types of evidence that help us find out about early people.

2. Describe how Stone Age people found food and shelter.

3. Copy the following statements and indicate whether they are **true** or **false**:
    a. Cave paintings provide useful evidence about the life and appearance of early people.
    b. The earliest people made tools and weapons from stone.
    c. The earliest evidence of human existence was found in Tanzania.
    d. The first farmers appeared around 12000 BC.

4. Why was the discovery of fire so important to Stone Age people?

Extended writing

1. In what ways did the development of farming change the lives of early people?

2. What evidence suggests that early people were not barbaric or uncivilised?

Stone Age people in Scotland

6500 BC	Mesolithic (Middle Stone Age) hunters settle in Scotland
4000 BC	Neolithic (New Stone Age) farmers arrive in Scotland
3100 BC–2500 BC	Skara Brae is occupied by Stone Age People
2000 BC	The rise of the Beaker People
2000 BC–600 BC	The Bronze Age

Mesolithic hunters

The earliest inhabitants of Scotland arrived about 8000 years ago. They were hunters and fishers and lived a **nomadic** existence (they moved camp regularly). The earliest Mesolithic settlement in Scotland is at Kinloch on the island of Rhum.

These people were attracted to Scotland by a number of factors. They could pick roots, berries and nuts for food. They could hunt animals like bears, boar, beavers, deer, wild cattle and horses. The long stretches of coasts, islands and rivers provided fish, shellfish, sea birds and seaweed.

The hunters lived in huts or tents. The site of the camp had to be near a source of water and have resources nearby. There was plenty of woodland to help build their camps as well as make weapons and tools. However, the most important use of wood was for fire. Most communities would have kept a fire burning not just for warmth and cooking but also to keep wild animals away.

Neolithic farmers

Source A

About 4000 BC new people came to Scotland from continental Europe via England. Although they were still Stone Age people they knew how to farm as well as how to hunt. They brought cows, sheep and pigs in their boats. They also brought wheat and barley seeds, which they planted. The best examples of Neolithic settlements are to be found in Orkney, Papa Westray and Shetland.

Evidence shows that, despite a more varied diet, life was hard and, in many cases, short. Bones found at a Neolithic burial site in South Ronaldsay indicate that many people died between the ages of 15 and 30. Only a very few people lived until they were 50.

Knap of Howar, a Neolithic settlement on Papa Westray. ▶

In 1850 a storm struck the island of Orkney and blew away some sand dunes, revealing the Stone Age settlement of Skara Brae. The most remarkable aspect of Skara Brae is that it has been so well preserved. Evidence shows that the settlement was abandoned in a hurry as people's possessions, including tools and jewellery, were left behind. Scientists believe that the settlement was established around 3100 BC and that the people left about 2500 BC.

Source B

Skara Brae.

Around 50 people lived in Skara Brae. There are seven huts: six of these would have been homes with the seventh providing a common area, possibly a kitchen or a workshop. The houses were linked by covered passageways.

The houses are constructed of stone slabs because there are no trees on Orkney. A typical house consists of a single room with very thick walls. The entrance is low and narrow so the inhabitants would have to get down on their hands and knees to enter. In the centre of the room is a large stone hearth. They had beds made from thin stone slabs and small cupboards for personal possessions. They also had cupboards for storing food and even a simple toilet.

The villagers of Skara Brae appear to have been self-sufficient: they provided their own food and made their own tools and pottery. The obvious organisation of the village and its similarity to other settlements in the Orkneys suggest that these were not primitive people.

The Beaker People

The Beaker People lived in Scotland before 2000 BC and are named after the style of pottery that they developed. It is possible that they were new arrivals to Scotland and brought this style with them. The Beaker People were the link between the Neolithic Age and the Bronze Age. Scotland's Bronze Age lasted from about 2000 BC to 600 BC. During this period people developed skills in making tools, weapons and shields from bronze. Bronze Age settlements had circular houses built with timber at the centre of large farms.

Questions

1. Put the following into chronological order:

The Beaker People	Skara Brae occupied by Stone Age people
Mesolithic hunters settle in Scotland	Neolithic farmers arrive in Scotland
Beginning of the Bronze Age	

2. Once you have put the people above in chronological order, draw a timeline of the early people in Scotland from the first settlers up to the Bronze Age.

3. How did the earliest people to come to Scotland provide food and shelter for themselves?

4. Where have archaeologists found the best evidence of Neolithic settlements in Scotland?

5. Describe the settlement at Skara Brae. Mention the location, layout, furniture and the materials used.

6. How was Skara Brae discovered? Can you think of a reason why the people left Skara Brae in such a hurry?

Extended writing

1. What hardships did Neolithic peoples have to face?

2. Using the school library, the local library or the Internet find out more about one of the following:

Neolithic Burial Sites	Skara Brae
The Standing Stones at Callanish in Lewis	The Beaker People

The great civilisation of Ancient Egypt began over 5000 years ago and continues to fascinate historians even today. Nearly 3000 years before the birth of Christ, the Egyptians had reached an advanced stage of civilisation: they had orderly government, a highly developed system of agriculture and had made great advances in science and medicine. In building and architecture, they had produced enormous stone structures and, most importantly, they had developed the art of writing. For over 3000 years, the Egypt of the **pharaohs** (the pharaoh was the ruler) remained strong and powerful, conquering neighbouring lands.

Many people believe that history itself really began with the Egyptians, as there is both written (or documentary) evidence and strong archaeological evidence about their lives and culture. Based on the work of Egyptian priests, who made lists of the pharaohs and the important events of their reigns, modern historians have grouped the many dynasties into three main periods when Egyptian civilisation flourished: the Old Kingdom, the Middle Kingdom and the New Kingdom.

Ancient Egypt. ▶

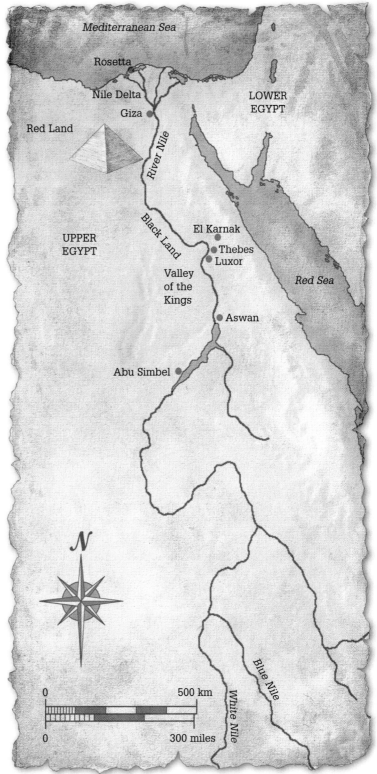

9

Timeline of Ancient Egypt

3100 BC – 2686 BC: Early Dynastic Period

Menes, the ruler of Upper Egypt, conquers Lower Egypt and unites the two kingdoms. This is the beginning of the First **Dynasty**. (A dynasty is a succession of rulers of the same line of descent.) During this period, the Egyptians develop a system of government and the art of writing.

2686 BC – 2181 BC: the period of the Old Kingdom

Imhotep designs and builds a new type of tomb for King Djoser: the famous Step Pyramid. It was 62 metres high. This is the beginning of the Pyramid Age, which reaches its peak with the building of three gigantic pyramids for the pharaohs Khufu, Khafre and Menkure at Giza. The Great Sphinx is also built at Giza in this period. Art and sculpture are highly developed and appreciated in this age.

2055 BC – 1650 BC: the Middle Kingdom

A period of economic expansion and prosperity under pharaohs Amenemhat and Sensuret. Major **irrigation** works (providing water for farms) are constructed, trade increases and the building of the largest temple of all, the Temple of Amen at El Karnak, begins. Art and literature continue to flourish in this period.

1550 BC – c.1100 BC: the New Kingdom

Egyptians learn the techniques of warfare and begin to conquer neighbouring lands. The empire reaches its peak under Thutmose III. With the wealth based on their empire the pharaohs of the New Kingdom build many large temples and pyramids, for example, the temples at El Karnak and Luxor, the tombs in the Valley of the Kings. Tutankhamun re-establishes Thebes as the capital of Egypt.

Source A

Ruins of the temple at El Karnak.

1100 BC – 30 BC: the Late Period

Extensive building projects exhaust Egypt's wealth and its power declines. Egypt is in turn invaded by the Ethiopians, the Assyrians and later conquered by the Persians under Alexander the Great. Despite the efforts of Cleopatra Egypt becomes a province of the Roman Empire in 30 BC.

Note: To the people of ancient Egypt their country was known as 'Kemet'; the name 'Egypt' was the Greek word for Kemet.

The River Nile

In the fifth century BC, Herodotus, a visiting Greek historian, described the country as 'the gift of the Nile'. Herodotus also said that 'there was no region in Egypt where the fruits of the soil could be harvested so easily' as in the Nile Delta in Lower Egypt.

The River Nile (the longest river in Africa: 6671 kilometres long) ran the length of the country and was vital to the development of the civilisation known as Ancient Egypt. Approximately 90 per cent of Egypt was covered by desert and was known as the 'Red Land'. In the very dry climate of Africa, the Nile provided water not just for drinking but also for growing crops. The majority of Egyptians lived along the banks of the Nile in the area known as the 'Kemet' or the 'Black Land'. Each year around July, when the snows on the mountains melted, the River Nile swelled and flooded its banks. The calendar and life in Ancient Egypt were both determined by this annual flood. The farmer's year was divided into three distinct periods or seasons: the flood, the growing period and the harvest.

The flood

Given the importance of the annual flood, the Ancient Egyptians tried to predict the size of the flood: if the floodwaters were too high then villages or settlements might be covered, too low and there might be food shortages. The Egyptians developed the nilometer, which measured the water levels along the River Nile at the beginning of the flood season. These measurements showed the levels the floodwaters would reach so that plans could be made.

The growing period

When the waters retreated in the summer heat they left behind silt that made the soil rich and fertile. This fertile strip was approximately ten kilometres wide. Then the farmers got to work sowing flax, barley and wheat. As the land in the valley of the Nile was so fertile it was possible to grow two crops in one year.

Irrigating the land

Given that the climate was hot and dry with no rain, it was essential that the farmers make the best possible use of the water from the Nile. Canals were cut to bring water to fields as far away from the riverbanks as possible: this is called irrigation. The use of the nilometer and the development of this irrigation system show that Ancient Egypt was an advanced civilisation.

To raise the water from the river to fill the canals, the Egyptians used the shaduf, introduced c.1500 BC. This was a long wooden pole with a bucket at one end and a counterbalance at the other. About 500 BC the Archimedes waterscrew was developed, and later people used water wheels driven by oxen. Even today Egyptian farmers still use the shaduf.

Source A

A shaduf in operation. ▲

The harvest

During this season the farmers began reaping using wooden sickles. The corn had to be threshed and winnowed and then stored under the watchful eye of a **scribe** (writer) who noted carefully how much grain had been produced. This also helped them to work out taxes. Evidence that Ancient Egypt was an advanced civilisation is again shown from the fact that the grain was stored on the orders of the pharaoh so that the people could be fed in times of shortage.

The River Nile: a 'motorway' of the Ancient World?

The main method of transport in Ancient Egypt was by boat along the River Nile. The earliest Egyptian boats were made from **papyrus** (a type of plant also used to make paper) but, gradually, wooden ships and barges were developed, which used sails and oars. The River Nile was important for trade as it was the main link between the different parts of the country; for example the stone to build the pyramids had to be transported upriver by barge.

Questions

1. How long was the River Nile?

2. When and why did the River Nile flood its banks?

3. In what way did the annual flood help the farmers of Ancient Egypt?

4. Describe and explain the use of the following:

nilometer
shaduf
irrigation canals

5. What were the main crops produced in Ancient Egypt?

6. List the many ways in which the Ancient Egyptians used the River Nile.

Extended writing

1. Herodotus described Egypt as 'the gift of the Nile'. Explain why the River Nile was so important to the development of the civilisation of Ancient Egypt.

2. What evidence is there to support the view that Ancient Egypt was an advanced civilisation?

5 Daily life in Ancient Egypt (1)

Today, new inventions and discoveries are made every year; new fads and fashions develop that affect everyday life. Through communications, migration and travel, many foreign cultures merge, forming new cultures. The Egyptians had their greatest creative period at the very beginning of their long history. After that, their way of living changed very little through the years.

Egyptian society was very organised and everyone had a part to play. At the top was the pharaoh. Below the pharaoh, the people were organised into three main classes: upper, middle and lower.

- The upper class consisted of the royal family, government officials, diplomats, high priests and priestesses, scribes and doctors.

- The middle class was made up of traders, merchants and craftsmen, like potters or jewellers.

- The lower class was the largest group of people and was made up of the unskilled workers who did the heavy work in the fields or in building the pyramids.

Pharaoh

Royal family
Priests
Doctors
Scribes

Traders
Craftsmen

Unskilled workers

The organisation of Egyptian society.

Egypt was protected by the sea on the north and by deserts to the east and west. Since the Egyptians could develop without fear of invasion, their interests were focused on their homes and families and on their work. Villages and towns were situated near the Nile because it was the chief highway as well as the only source of water. One village, Deir el-Medina, lay buried under the sands for centuries until it was discovered in the nineteenth century. During the twentieth century, Deir el-Medina was excavated by archaeologists and has provided a lot of information about the lives of ordinary Egyptians.

What was life like for the upper class in Ancient Egypt?

Even the rich lived in houses made of mud brick, though their houses were much larger than those of the poor. Windows were small, high openings covered with loosely woven matting to keep out the heat and glare of the sun. Everywhere houses were crowded close together to leave more space for farmland. Usually houses were built back to back to save space. Some opened onto a narrow street; others faced a small walled garden.

The walls of the houses were decorated with bright **frescoes** (wall paintings). Straw matting and rugs covered the floors. Lamps were saucers of oil with a floating wick. Rich people had beds, chairs, and stools but no real dining tables. They kept their clothes and linen sheets in box chests or in baskets.

Egyptian fashions

The members of Egypt's upper classes spent a lot of their time on their appearance. They bathed with soda and then rubbed perfumed oil into the skin. Men shaved with a bronze razor. They cut their hair short and wore wigs. Women also wore wigs or added false braids to their own hair. They had combs and hairpins, and mirrors of polished bronze or silver.

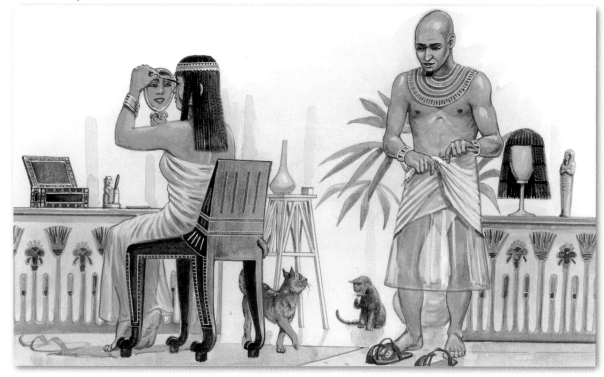

Egyptian men and women taking care of their appearance.

Both men and women darkened their eyelids with black eye make-up called kohl. Women rouged their cheeks and lips and stained their nails with henna. Men usually wore only a kilt-like skirt. Women wore white dresses with bands over the shoulders. Both men and women wore jewellery – collars and necklaces, strings of beads, bracelets, anklets, earrings, and finger rings.

What was life like for peasants and craftsmen in Ancient Egypt?

Although there were many different occupations in Ancient Egypt most people worked as farm workers. Men did the ploughing and reaping while women sowed the seeds and were involved in the harvesting.

After the crops were harvested, the pharaoh could call on the people to work on irrigation schemes, to quarry stone or to build tombs and temples. Their only pay was grain from the state granaries, oil, fish, vegetables, and clothing.

The craftsmen and artists had an easier life than the farm workers. They worked in shops close to the palace of the pharaoh or on the estates of priests and nobles.

Smiths forged bronze tools and weapons and made fine copper and bronze dishes. Goldsmiths and silversmiths made household goods as well as extravagant jewellery. Stonemasons ground out vases, jars, bowls and platters. The stonemasons also created great statues such as the Sphinx.

Potters made clay vessels on a potter's wheel, which they often decorated with a blue glaze. Women wove fabrics of linen for clothing and for tapestries to decorate the houses of the rich. Egypt had little timber. Cedar and cypress were imported and used by cabinetmakers to make chairs and couches.

The River Nile was a vital transport link so shipbuilding was a very important occupation. Shipbuilders made vessels with curving hulls and tall sails and cargo ships to sail to foreign lands. Paper workers took the papyrus reeds gathered from the Nile marshes, split them, and pasted them to make a pale yellow writing paper.

15

Questions

1. Complete the following table – which class did these people belong to?

scribes   royal family   farmers   labourers   artists   stonemasons   goldsmiths   silversmiths   potters   cabinet makers   ship builders   paper workers

Upper Class	Middle Class	Lower Class

2. Explain how the discovery of the village of Deir el-Medina has helped us to find out about the lives of ordinary Egyptians.

3. What was life like for rich Egyptians? Make notes under the following headings: homes, furniture, clothes, jewellery, appearance.

4. Describe the main jobs done by lower class Egyptians.

5. What was unusual about the way the peasants were paid?

The fertile mud left by the annual Nile flood allowed the Egyptians to grow barley and wheat. These crops provided the staple Egyptian diet of bread and beer. Given the fertility of the Nile valley the Egyptians could also grow various vegetables such as garlic, onions, leeks, lettuce and different kinds of beans. The very hot and dry climate of Egypt made it difficult to grow citrus fruits but they did produce grapes (to make wine), dates, figs, pomegranates and cucumbers. Most Egyptians therefore enjoyed a healthy diet of fruit and vegetables. Fish from the Nile was eaten mainly by the poor, while the rich also enjoyed roast meat and poultry.

Preserving, cooking and eating food

In a very hot climate preserving food is very important: grain was stored in large granaries; within households food, water, beer and wine were stored in large pottery jars. Duck and fish were dried in the sun or the fish might be salted. Egyptians cooked their food in a clay oven or over an open fire. Most kitchens were equipped with a large oven made from bricks or clay.

The Egyptians loved good food and drink. At a banquet the richer guests would sit on carved and decorated chairs, and those of lesser importance on stools. Knives and forks were unknown so the Egyptians ate with their fingers. Between courses, servants would bring scented water for the guests to wash their fingers. The pharaoh would have a servant to wash his hands

Source A

A tomb painting showing an Egyptian banquet.

between each course. The various courses might include meat roasted with spices, even fillet steak, or wildfowl from the Nile marshes and this would be washed down with wine.

During the banquet, guests would be entertained by musicians, dancing girls and acrobats. The musicians had a variety of instruments including flutes, harps and castanets.

—— *Entertainment*

The Egyptians played a number of board games, some of which we still play today. The most popular board game was 'Senet': this game symbolised the eternal struggle between good and evil. The aim of the game was to reach the kingdom of the god Osiris and with each throwstick you might land on a square that gave you an advantage like 'beauty' or 'power' or land on a square depicting some peril or disaster. An indication of the popularity of Senet can be found in the treasures of Tutankhamun, which contained four ornate Senet boards. Another board game played by the Egyptians was called 'Snake'. This was played on a circular board and the winner was the first player to get their counter to the centre of the coiled serpent's head.

Childhood was short for young Egyptians as girls married around the age of 12 and boys at the age of 14. However, they still enjoyed toys and games. Popular toys included dolls, balls and model animals. Leapfrog and tug-of-war were also played by boys and girls. Some Egyptian children kept pets, most commonly dogs or cats. However, some children had more exotic pets such as monkeys or gazelles.

17

Questions ——————————————

1. Describe the diet of a poor Egyptian.

2. How did the Egyptians preserve and cook food?

3. What was life like for rich Egyptians? Make notes under the following headings: diet, banquets, entertainment, games.

4. Why was childhood quite short for Egyptian children?

5. List the toys and games enjoyed by Egyptian children.

6. Explain how the following board games were played: Senet and Snake. Do these board games remind you of any games still played today?

Extended writing

1. Using your research notes from Question 3 in both this section and the last section, and any other appropriate sources, write a report on 'What was life like in Ancient Egypt?'. If possible, you could include pictures or diagrams.

The Egyptians believed in many gods. Each area once had its own gods but other gods were worshipped throughout Egypt. Given that Egyptian civilisation lasted thousands of years some gods were more popular in different eras. When the country was united, the people worshipped the pharaoh, too.

The Creation Legend

According to the Egyptian account of creation, only the ocean existed at first. Then Ra, the sun, came out of an egg (a flower, in some versions) that appeared on the surface of the water. Ra brought forth four children, the gods Shu and Geb and the goddesses Tefnut and Nut. Shu and Tefnut became the atmosphere. They stood on Geb, who became the earth, and raised up Nut, who became the sky. Ra ruled over all and became known as Re, or Amun Re. Geb and Nut later had two sons, Seth and Osiris, and two daughters, Isis and Nephthys. Osiris succeeded Ra as king of the earth, helped by Isis, his sister-wife. Seth, however, hated his brother and killed him. Isis then **embalmed** her husband's body with the help of the god Anubis, who became the god of embalming. The powerful charms of Isis resurrected Osiris, who became king of the netherworld, the land of the dead. Horus, who was the son of Osiris and Isis, later defeated Seth in a great battle and became king of the earth.

— *Egyptian Gods and Goddesses*

Many Egyptian gods represented things common in the lives of the people. Cows were important in the Egyptian economy so the cow goddess, Hathor, was particularly popular; she was also the goddess of music and love. The jackal-headed god Anubis supervised embalming and was the god of **mummification** (see page 20 for more information on embalming and mummification). As the beak of the ibis (a type of bird) resembled a crescent moon the ibis came to represent Thoth, the moon god and god of truth. The Egyptians believed that Thoth was the patron of the scribes and had given Egyptians writing, medicine and mathematics.

Of all the gods and goddesses, three of the most important were Horus, Isis and Osiris. Carvings often show Horus, the falcon-headed god, hovering just behind the pharaoh to give him divine protection. He was also painted on mummy-cases (coffins), with his wings protectively outspread to help the dead person through the underworld. Respect for the dead and belief in a life after death played a very important part in Egyptian religion.

— *Isis and Osiris*

Perhaps the most interesting of the gods and goddesses of Egypt were the sister and brother, Isis and Osiris (see the Creation Legend). Egyptians believed that Osiris used his divine influence to make the crops grow tall. Osiris was the god who judged all men when they died. Isis was the goddess of and protector of women.

Re and Amun

The most important god was Re, the sun god, who was believed to take on different forms at different times of the day. Amun was the god of air and of Thebes: his name means hidden. During the New Kingdom, when Thebes became the capital of Egypt, Amun merged with Re to become the principal god, Amun-Re. It was believed that Amun-Re handed the great sword of conquest to the warrior pharaohs like Thutmose III.

According to the priests, the pharaoh represented Amun (or Amun-Re), the supreme being. The many temples built to the different gods throughout the country were looked after by large numbers of priests. People made gifts to the temples of their chosen gods but as the temples paid no taxes, the priests who looked after them enjoyed all this wealth. The chief priest of a great temple had enormous power and wealth.

Some people felt the priests were becoming far too powerful. Akhenaten, the pharaoh before Tutankhamun, tried to break their power by starting a new type of religion but this failed.

Source A

Isis. ▲

Source B

Osiris. ▲

19

Questions

1. Copy and complete the following table about the gods and goddesses worshipped in Ancient Egypt.

God	Image	God of...?
Hathor	Cow	Goddess of Love & Music
Thoth		
Anubis		
Osiris		
Isis		
Horus		
Re		
Amun		
Amun-Re		

2. Explain why the ancient Egyptians worshipped so many different gods.

3. Explain why priests became such powerful people in Ancient Egypt.

Ever since archaeologists began to explore and excavate the tombs and pyramids of Ancient Egypt, people have become fascinated by Egyptian beliefs about death and the afterlife. The image of the 'mummy' has become as familiar as the pyramids as a representation of Ancient Egypt.

The Egyptians believed in an afterlife and that the spirit of a dead person travelled to a kind of heavenly Egypt where it could live forever. Many important ceremonies had to be carried out when someone died: the most important process involved preserving the body of the dead person to make sure it did not decay. Dead people were provided with all the food, furniture, tools and riches, which they would need for the afterlife.

Mummification

Mummification is the word used to describe the process of preserving a body by embalming it. Organs such as the lungs, liver and intestines were removed from the body and placed in special containers called Canopic jars. The brain was extracted through the nostrils. The heart was left in the body. The body was then washed in oils and perfumes before being covered with a salt called natron to dry it. After this the body was packed with linen, sawdust and spices and then wrapped in linen bandages. The whole process of mummification took about 70 days to complete. Good luck charms were often placed within the layers of bandages or even spells written on papyrus. Many Egyptians had a Book of the Dead buried with them, which contained over 200 spells, believing that its magical text would help their souls to the Celestial Fields (heaven). Spell 31 for example, was to guard the body against demons in the form of reptiles.

A mask showing a likeness of the dead person was placed on the head of the mummy and then it was put in the sarcophagus (or coffin) before being buried in a tomb.

Source A

Get away from me!
Stay away, you evil one!
O you who would speak against this magic of mine,
No crocodile .... will take it away from me!

An extract from Spell 31.

Embalming

The Egyptians were very skilled at embalming; the soles of the feet of mummies, when unwrapped after as much as 3000 years, are often still soft and elastic. Historians estimate that by AD 700, when the practice had died out, the Egyptians had embalmed approximately 730 million bodies. Although many were destroyed or disintegrated in the tropical heat of northern Africa, a large number of mummies were preserved; archaeologists estimate that several million are still preserved in undiscovered tombs and burial places.

Source B

▲ *This picture comes from the* **Book of the Dead** *buried with the nobleman Ani and his wife. The jackal-headed god Anubis is weighing their souls against the Feather of Truth, to see if they are worthy to pass, while Thoth, god of truth, records the result. Behind him is the Devourer, a crocodile-headed monster who devours any souls who fail the test.*

Questions

1. What beliefs did the Egyptians hold about death?

2. Why did the Egyptians believe that the dead person's possessions should be buried along with them?

3. Paired Work: Mummification.
With your partner discuss:

   a. why the Egyptians 'mummified' the body of a dead person
   b. what Canopic jars were used for
   c. what natron was used for
   d. the use of linen bandages
   e. good luck charms and spells
   f. the mask, the sarcophagus and the tomb.

4. Based on your discussions in Question 3 write a report on the process of mummification using all the words mentioned in Question 3.

5. What evidence do we have that the Egyptians were very good at embalming and mummification?

6. According to the Egyptian Book of the Dead what happened to the dead person when they came face to face with Anubis and Thoth?

Extended writing

1. Using the school library or your local library try and find out about the 'curse of the mummy'.

9 Pyramids

As we have already learned, the ancient Egyptians believed in an afterlife and regarded the pharaoh as a god. Therefore a dead pharaoh needed an especially grand tomb. The pyramids were tombs built for the pharaohs.

The earliest pyramids had stepped sides: these probably represented a stairway that enabled the dead pharaoh to climb towards the stars and the sun to join his fellow gods.

Imhotep, a chief architect, designed and built the tomb of King Djoser: the famous Step Pyramid in the desert at Saqqara. Built in 2680 BC this is the world's oldest pyramid. ▶

The Pyramids at Giza

Among the most famous of the pyramids were those built on the west bank of the Nile near the town of Giza more than 4500 years ago. They were built for three pharaohs: Khufu, Khafre and Menkaure. The Great Pyramid, built for Khufu, was the largest ever made: it was made with over 2 million blocks of limestone and when finished it was 146 metres high, making it the tallest building ever at that time. Near Giza is the Great Sphinx: it has the body of a crouching lion and the head of a king, probably Khafre. Egyptians believed that the Sphinx was guarding the way to the Great Pyramid.

The Great Sphinx at Giza. ▶

The pyramids at Giza were the first of the 'Seven Wonders of the Ancient World': when Tutankhamun (see page 25) ruled Egypt the Giza Pyramids were already more than a thousand years old; when Cleopatra (see page 24) ruled Egypt the Giza Pyramids were already more than 2500 years old.

Building a pyramid

It took hundreds of thousands of pieces of stone to build a pyramid. Quarrying all this stone and moving it to the site was an enormous task carried out by thousands of workers. Some of the limestone blocks had to be transported by barge along the River Nile. Granite, used in the interior of the pyramid, had to be brought upriver from Aswan, a journey of nearly 2000 km. Once delivered to the site, teams of labourers used ropes and wooden rollers to drag the heavy blocks up slopes of mud brick, until they could be placed on the structure of the pyramid.

The successful building of the pyramids is a sign of Egypt's peace, prosperity and stability. Only a very secure country could afford the time and men for such enormous projects. The building of the pyramids required an army of labourers as well as specialist craftsmen.

As the pharaohs were buried with a variety of treasures to take to the afterlife, the pyramids became a target for thieves or tomb robbers. To stop robbers, the pyramid builders hid the entrances, sealed internal passages with huge blocks of stone or created false passages to fool tomb robbers.

The Valley of the Kings

As the pyramids seemed such an obvious target for the tomb robbers, a new type of tomb for pharaohs was developed from around 2150 BC. Later pharaohs were buried in tombs cut into rock. The most sacred burial place was the Valley of the Kings, a remote place to the west of the River Nile opposite the city of Thebes. Some of the tombs in the Valley of the Kings were cut into the cliffside, others were built underground. However, despite elaborate security precautions all of the tombs in the Valley of the Kings were robbed, except one ... Tutankhamun's tomb (see Case Study, page 25).

The Egyptians also built many temples in honour of the gods and they were so well built many of them have survived. One of the most famous temples was at Abu Simbel, built on the orders of Rameses II. Four enormous statues of Rameses guard the entrance to the temple.

Questions

1. What was the purpose of the pyramids?

2. What is distinctive about the pyramid of King Djoser?

3. For which pharaohs were the Giza pyramids built?

4. Explain why one of the Giza pyramids is known as the Great Pyramid.

5. Describe how the pyramids were built: you should mention such things as materials, workers, craftsmen, time.

6. What security measures were taken to protect the contents of the pyramids and why were these necessary?

Extended writing

1. Using the school library, your local library or the Internet find out more about the pyramids. Write a report on 'The importance of the pyramids'. Include illustrations and/or drawings.

For over 3000 years, Egypt was ruled by pharaohs (the word 'pharaoh' means great house). The pharaoh was the most important and powerful person in the country. To the ancient Egyptians the pharaoh was a god who had come to live among them. To ensure that his children would have the blood of gods the pharaoh often married his sister or half-sister. The pharaoh was the commander of the army, decided the laws of the country and was in charge of the treasury.

Ancient Egypt had a population of approximately five million people. To help the pharaoh rule he had a large number of advisers and scribes. His most important adviser was the vizier who was the second most important man in Egypt. The vizier and his officials ensured that everyone paid their taxes.

— *Famous pharaohs*

- Menes is famous because he was the first of the pharaohs who united Upper and Lower Egypt in c. 3200 BC.

- Thutmose III (1487 BC–1424 BC) became pharaoh during the period of the New Kingdom and was regarded as the greatest of the warrior pharaohs. Thutmose III was a very successful military commander and expanded the Egyptian empire by conquering Palestine and Syria.

- Tutankhamun came to the throne of Egypt around the year 1332 BC, when he was only a boy. His rule lasted about ten years but he restored some order after Akhenaten, the pharaoh before Tutankhamun, had caused chaos by trying to start a new type of religion. Despite his relatively short rule Tutankhamun has become one of the best-known rulers of Ancient Egypt (see Case Study).

- Rameses II ruled for over 60 years (1290 BC–1224 BC) and was responsible for defeating the Hittites in 1285 BC and for the building of many monuments, most notably the temple at Abu Simbel. Many large statues of Rameses II have survived.

- Cleopatra (69 BC–30 BC) was one of the few women to become pharaoh. She ruled Egypt during the first century BC when the country was under threat from the powerful Roman Empire. She tried to establish an alliance with Rome to prevent Egypt being swallowed up by the Romans. However, when her armies were eventually defeated by the Romans, Cleopatra committed suicide and Egypt became a province of the Roman Empire.

Source A

Cleopatra. ▲

Source B

It is my firm opinion that in the Valley of the Kings there are no more unknown tombs.

Belzoni, an Italian explorer, 1817.

Many archaeologists agreed with Belzoni with two notable exceptions. Lord Carnarvon, a rich Englishman, had become interested in Egyptian archaeology and had hired a young archaeologist, Howard Carter, to excavate in the Valley of the Kings. After many years of searching with little success, Carter persuaded Carnarvon to pay for one more dig. In 1922 he began to excavate near the remains of several ancient stone huts. One of Carter's labourers found a stone step and this turned out to be the first step towards a hidden passageway leading to the tomb of Tutankhamun. Carter sent a telegram to Lord Carnarvon, who immediately set off for Egypt. On 26th November, 1922, the decisive moment came. Carter removed some stones from the doorway, held up a candle and looked through.

At first Carter could see nothing.

Source C

But presently, as my eyes grew accustomed to the light, details of the room within emerged slowly from the mist, strange animals, statues, and gold – everywhere the glint of gold.

Carter's description as he looked into the tomb.

The tomb chambers were filled with an enormous number of magnificent objects and treasures, which the young pharaoh could use in the afterlife. Tutankhamun was buried in an inner coffin made of solid gold and with him were jewellery, amulets and most famously a stunning gold portrait mask (see left). In the outer rooms of the tomb was a large variety of treasures and objects from Ancient Egypt including a chariot, weapons, clothes and furniture.

Compared with other famous pharaohs Tutankhamun was of little importance in early history; however, thanks to Carter's discovery of his tomb and its treasures in the twentieth century, thousands of years after his life and death, Tutankhamun has achieved celebrity status.

Source D

◀ *Tutankhamun's gold mask.*

Questions

1. Matching Exercise.

Match the individuals in Group A with the correct statement or definition in Group B

Group A	Group B
pharaoh	united Upper and Lower Egypt
Menes	committed suicide when Egypt became a province of the Roman Empire
vizier	most important and powerful person in the country
Cleopatra	nineteenth-century Italian explorer
Rameses II	ruled for over 60 years and built the Temple of Abu Simbel
Thutmose III	very successful military commander
Belzoni	chief assistant to the pharaoh in running the country

2. In what way does the evidence in Source B disagree with the view held by Lord Carnarvon?

3. List and describe the objects discovered by Howard Carter.

4. Groupwork:

In your group discuss the thoughts and feelings of Howard Carter and Lord Carnarvon in November 1922. Each group should complete one of the following exercises:

   a. Imagine you are Howard Carter and complete a diary covering the main events of November 1922. Try to convey his feelings and some details of the actual discovery.
   b. Imagine you are Howard Carter and write a letter home describing the main events of November 1922. Try to convey his feelings and some details of the actual discovery.
   c. Imagine you are Lord Carnarvon and write a letter to *The Times* describing the importance of the discovery of Tutankhamun's tomb.
   d. Write a newspaper front page for *The Times* describing the discovery of Tutankhamun's tomb.

5. Each group should report back or display their work to the whole class.

Extended writing

1. 'The pharaoh was the most important and powerful person in ancient Egypt'. What evidence can you find to support the above statement?

2. 'The treasure dug up is not gold, but history … every day there is a new light on the past.' British archaeologist, William Petrie, from his book *Digging for Dreams*.

Explain how the discovery of Tutankhamun's tomb provided

   a. gold

   b. a new light on the past.

The legacy of Ancient Egypt

Ancient Egypt was one of the first great civilisations of the world and it influenced many other people and cultures which developed later, especially the Greeks and the Romans. African and Arab people also take great pride in the advanced civilisation of Ancient Egypt. The Egyptians were the first people to develop the art of writing and this had a great influence on succeeding civilisations. **Egyptology**, the study of Ancient Egypt, became a subject in its own right.

As Egyptian scribes recorded such detailed accounts of everyday life, as well as major events, historians have a large amount of written evidence that has survived. Archaeologists have also provided us with a clear picture of Ancient Egypt and its people, through excavations of buildings and monuments. The pyramids and the tombs in the Valley of the Kings contain elaborate wall paintings, which illustrate what life was like at the time of the pharaohs. Archaeologists have also been able to study and learn from the many artefacts found in the tombs or everyday objects that were simply thrown away by ancient Egyptians and have been preserved by the hot, dry climate and the desert sands.

The Rosetta Stone

The word we use for Egyptian writing is **hieroglyphics**, which originally meant 'sacred carvings' and can best be described as 'picture writing'. As hieroglyphic writing was difficult to do quickly scribes developed a shorthand form called **hieratic**, which was used for letters, stories and business contracts. **Demotic** was an even quicker script developed for legal documents.

In 1799 a soldier in the army of the French leader Napoleon discovered a broken stone near Rosetta in the Nile delta. The stone was covered in hieroglyphics and other forms of writing, both Egyptian and Greek. In 1822 a French scholar, Jean-Francois Champollion, succeeded in deciphering the Rosetta Stone. He worked out that the stone recorded the coronation of Ptolemy V in three different languages and by translating the Greek inscription he was able to decipher hieroglyphics for the first time. This breakthrough meant that scholars, archaeologists and historians could now more fully understand the history of Ancient Egypt.

Source A

Hieroglyphics carved into stone. ▲

Modern Egypt

Historians often look at the differences and similarities in the lifestyles of people from different periods in time. Many people living in Egypt today have a way of life not that different from people living in Ancient Egypt. For example, farmers living near the Nile still depend on the floods, though the flood is now controlled by the massive Aswan Dam making life less uncertain. Farmers still use similar methods and tools, such as the shaduf, and even their homes are still often made from sun-dried bricks.

Modern Egypt attracts many visitors, many of whom want to see the magnificence of the pyramids and the Valley of the Kings. People remain fascinated by the Ancient Egyptians partly because of the survival of so much evidence about their lives and time, and partly because there is still much we do not know, which adds to the continuing sense of mystery which surrounds the pyramids, tombs and mummies.

Source B

A tomb painting showing everyday life for Ancient Egyptians. ▶

Questions

1. Why was the 'breaking of the code' of the Rosetta Stone so important to historians?

2. Explain why the work of scribes has been so useful for historians.

3. Oliver Cromwell, who ruled England 1649–58 once asked an artist to paint his portrait exactly as he was, 'warts and all'. Describe how Egyptian artists showed the pharaohs. Explain how the image of the pharaoh was not 'warts and all'.

4. Historical evidence: why do we know so much about Ancient Egypt?

Extended writing

1. As an individual or as part of a group choose ONE of the following aspects of life in Ancient Egypt:

   You should research the topic by using class textbooks, the school library, your local library or the Internet.

The pharaohs	The Pyramids
Religion and the afterlife	The River Nile
Tutankhamun	Art and writing
Everyday life	

Who were the Celts?

Where did the ancient Celts come from?

Today when people speak of the
Celtic nations they usually mean
Ireland, Scotland, Wales, Cornwall,
Brittany in France and possibly
Galicia in Spain. However, the
ancient Celts spread much further.
At their strongest, around about
300 BC, their lands stretched across
much of Europe, from Scotland and
Ireland in the northwest to Turkey
in the southeast, from the Baltic Sea
to the Mediterranean. The name
'Celt' is applied to the various
peoples and tribes who spoke
similar languages and followed the
same way of life.

The power of the early Celts was
based on their strength as horse-
riding warriors. They loved to go on
raids, attacking and plundering
neighbours or other Celtic tribes.
Sometimes they would go off to
attack more distant foreign peoples.
There were different reasons for
going on raids:

- to gain precious goods, animals,
  food or other riches
- because they enjoyed fighting
- to practise and develop the skills
  of warfare and horse riding.

Celts on a raid
(see also p.38).

The early Celts of Central Europe lived in France, Germany, Austria and
the Alps. These early Celts are sometimes known as the Hallstatt Celts,
after their settlement in Austria. They became quite wealthy through
trade in salt, copper and iron ore. Iron could be used to make strong
weapons and tools. Salt could be used to preserve food and in the
making of simple remedies or medicines.

The Celts were established in settlements throughout Europe and were
a formidable force until the rise of the Roman Empire. Most of the
Celtic tribes were eventually conquered by the Romans, though some
managed to escape and their way of life survived in parts of Wales,
Scotland and Ireland.

How do we know about the Celts?

The earliest written reference to the existence of the Celts was by the Greek historian Herodotus in the fifth century BC. As far as we know the Celts themselves did not write books but evidence about their way of life has survived.

We can find out about them from the many objects which they left behind. Hidden coins, weapons thrown into rivers, dropped brooches, chariot wheels buried with dead chiefs – all these objects tell us something about the Celts.

Although the Celts left no written records about themselves, Greek and Roman writers and historians have described the Celtic way of life. One of the most detailed descriptions of the Celts is by Julius Caesar in his book, *The Gallic Wars*. We need to be very careful when we read the Roman evidence about the Celts for two reasons:

● the Romans and the Celts were at war for over 200 years

● the Romans considered the Celts to be uncivilised barbarians.

The Roman accounts of the Celts could possibly be described as 'History written by the winners'.

Archaeologists have discovered other evidence about the Celts: settlements, hill-forts, walls, fields and villages. Using objects discovered, archaeological evidence and written evidence, we can build up a picture of what the Celts were like.

The Celts come to Britain and Ireland

Greek and Celtic travellers, as far back as the fifth and sixth centuries BC, referred to the 'Pretanic' Islands and to the islands of Albion and Ierne. Albion and Ierne are old Celtic or Irish words for Britain and Ireland. With the arrival of the Romans the 'Pretanic' Islands became Britannia and the people Britanni.

The Celts left their homelands in central Europe and began arriving in the islands of Britain and Ireland possibly as early as 700 BC. Due to the regular wars between Celtic tribes and later against the Romans, many of the Celtic settlers in Britain were fleeing from war or the Romans. Originally they settled mainly in the south and east of England but gradually they moved north and west. The Celts brought with them their knowledge and skills in farming and the use of iron tools and weapons.

As the Romans conquered Britain the defeated Celts fled west into Wales and Cornwall or further north into Scotland. Not all Celts were threatened by invaders. Parts of Britain and Ireland have been Celtic for more than two thousand years.

The Celts settled in tribes in different parts of the British Isles. ▼

Questions

1. Put the following events into chronological order:

the Celts are at war with the Romans

the Hallstatt Celts begin to mine salt and iron ore

the Romans drive the Celts out of southern Britain

the Celts begin to settle in Britain and Ireland

2. In which areas did the Celts settle?

3. At their strongest how far did the Celtic lands stretch?

4. Evidence about the Celts: list examples of evidence about the Celts under the following headings:

Objects	Archaeological	Written

5. When and why did the Celts come to Britain and Ireland?

6. Why did the Celtic way of life go into decline?

Extended writing

1. Explain why the early Celts were a powerful and wealthy people. You should mention: trade, raids, salt and iron ore.

2. Making judgements about evidence: why do we have to be careful in using the written accounts of the Celts?

Celtic society

The Celts who settled in Britain lived in tribes, each tribe having a chieftain. From Roman writings, we know that the Celts divided their society into three main groups: the nobles and warriors, farmers and learned men. The last group included doctors, bards, metalworkers and druids.

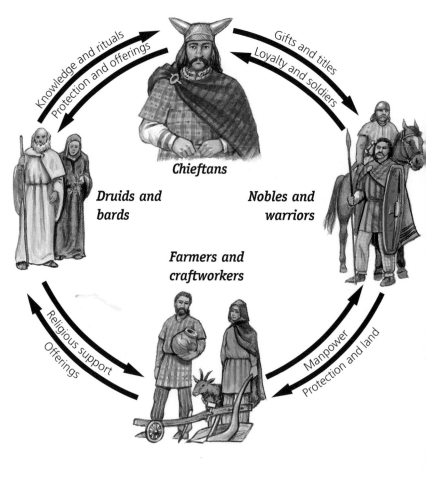

The organisation of Celtic society.

The nobles

The role of the king (or sometimes queen) was to lead men in battle and to protect the members of the tribe. High-ranking nobles were expected to support the chief and they had their own bands of warriors. The chief and the warriors provided the members of the tribe with land and protection. In return the tribes people paid taxes.

The Druids

The Druids were highly respected. They had the responsibility of learning and memorising the tribe's religion, laws, history and poetry. This meant that storytelling was very important, as all this knowledge was stored in their memories. According to Roman evidence the Druids also performed sacrifices to the gods. The remains of human sacrifices have been found preserved in peat bogs: two good examples are Tolland Man and Lindow Man.

Tollund Man was discovered in a peat bog in Denmark and Lindow Man in England. In each case police initially thought that they had discovered the body of someone recently murdered. Further investigations by scientists and archaeologists suggested that each body had been a victim of a ritual sacrifice of the type carried out by the Iron Age Celts. Both victims had suffered a violent death. Analysis of the contents of Lindow Man's stomach revealed he had eaten grains of mistletoe pollen mixed with a simple grain cake shortly before his death. This suggests a link to the Druids who carried out these ceremonies.

The Druids are concerned with the worship of the gods and give rulings on all religious questions ... They have the right to decide disputes, pass judgement in criminal and murder cases and can ban a person from attending religious ceremonies or sacrifices.

Druids, or Celtic priests, were especially important people, as Julius Caesar, Gallic Wars, confirms.

Bards

Bards were singers or poets and were very popular figures in Celtic society. The bards used words and songs to celebrate tribal successes. Poems told stories of great victories or daring raids. Songs were sung in tribute to dead chieftains or heroes.

Farmers

Farmers were also important as they produced food while craftsmen provided essential goods like tools and weapons as well as jewellery. Among the craftsmen the blacksmith was the most important – his craft was regarded as almost supernatural. At the bottom of Celtic society were labourers and slaves who did the hard and menial jobs.

33

Celtic settlements

Forts

Although the various Celtic tribes that settled in Britain and Ireland shared a language and a way of life, there were often conflicts between tribes. They built forts of earth and wood, or in some cases stone. In England, Wales and Ireland the Celts built hill forts for defence. Their position at the top of hills meant that defenders could see their enemies approaching and be prepared for an attack.

In Scotland and Ireland the Celts built round stone houses called 'duns' and round towers of stone

Source B

Maiden Castle in Dorset. ▼

called 'brochs'. Many towns and villages, even some cities, in Scotland and Ireland have the prefix 'dun' in their names. This means that there must have been a Celtic stone fort on the original site of these towns and villages.

The Celtic hill fort was a centre of social organisation. The Celts living in the fort would probably be chiefs and their families with some warriors for protection. Within the Celtic forts there would have been various buildings and workshops.

Source C

Chysauster in Cornwall. ▲

Villages

Outside the fort there were fields for growing crops and grazing animals. Not all Celts lived in forts: many lived in houses, farms and villages. The remains of a small Celtic village can be seen at Chysauster in Cornwall.

The people living in villages outside the fort grew their own food and made their own tools and clothes. They would only have gone to the fort in time of danger. They also paid taxes to the chief for the use of the land in the form of farm produce such as crops or meat.

Iron played an important part in Celtic life. Farmers had some tools made from iron, which helped them to produce enough food for themselves as well as some to sell. Corn was exported from Britain before the Roman conquest, showing that the Celtic farmers were producing more than they needed. The farmers produced grain and various vegetables and also kept cattle, sheep and pigs.

34

Questions

1. List the main groups in Celtic society in order of importance.

2. What was the role of a Celtic king or chieftain?

3. 'Druids, or Celtic priests, were especially important people in Celtic society.' List two pieces of evidence to support this statement.

4. Why were each of the following important members of a Celtic tribe?

   Farmers   Craftsmen   Bards

5. List the various types of evidence that have survived from the time of the Celts in Britain.

6. Why did the Celts build forts?

Extended writing

1. What was life like for the Celtic farmers living in villages away from the fort?

2. Research: using an atlas find as many places as you can in Scotland and Ireland that begin with the prefix 'dun'.

The Celts in Scotland

What were Celtic houses like?

Celtic houses were made from local materials. Where trees were plentiful, houses had wooden walls and thatched roofs. If there were not enough trees, the walls were built of stone. Inside there was usually just one big room, in which the whole family lived, cooked, ate and slept. Everyone gathered around the fire in the centre, for heat and light.

Brochs

The style of housing used by the Celts varies in different parts of Scotland. In the north and northwest the main type of housing was the broch. In the west, Argyll and Galloway the Celts lived in duns and in the east they built forts. In the north of Scotland and on the Scottish islands, there are many examples of stone tower-houses or brochs, probably built around the last two centuries BC and the first century AD.

This Broch has an inner and an outer wall, with a space in between. There are stairs inside the space, leading to upper levels. Inside the broch, a ledge sticks out of the wall about two metres above the ground. This supports an upper floor. With high walls and no windows the houses must have been very dark inside. ▼

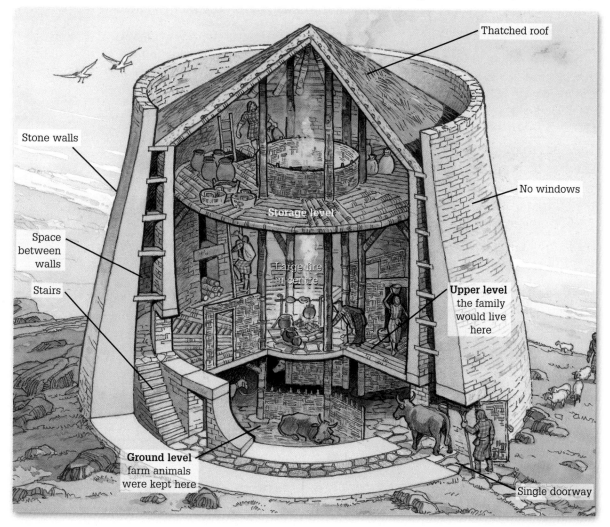

Thatched roof

Stone walls

No windows

Storage level

Space between walls

Large fire in centre

Stairs

Upper level the family would live here

Ground level farm animals were kept here

Single doorway

Some archaeologists believe that the ground floor was used for storage and for sheltering animals in winter. They think that people lived on the upper floor. No one can be sure of the truth and there is still a lot of disagreement among archaeologists about the way that the Scottish Celts lived. The best surviving example of a broch is on Mousa, a tiny island off Shetland.

The people who lived in the brochs must have believed they were well protected against attack. However, if the attackers were prepared to be patient and mount a long siege, then the occupants might have run out of food or water, forcing them to surrender. In the event of an attack it would not be possible to bring all the farm animals into the broch, which could allow the attackers to steal them.

Brochs were often built near water or a well. This may have been to ensure a supply of fresh water. It may also have been because early Celts exploring Scotland or looking for places to settle often travelled by sea rather than by land.

Duns and roundhouses

Duns were less substantial than brochs and had only one storey. The duns were large stone house circles usually built on high ground to make them look more important. They had walls of stone and wooden roofs covered by thatch.

Stone roundhouses were built in the north and west because there was plenty of stone available. In other areas the Celts built roundhouses of timber. In the Scottish Highlands, some people lived on man-made islands called crannogs, in the middle of lochs and rivers.

Crannogs

The Celts must have built crannogs as a form of security against attack by enemies or as protection against the many wild animals, like wolves and bears, which roamed Scotland. Crannogs were made by driving wooden posts into the bottom of the loch. Rocks, branches and turf were dropped between the posts. These formed a solid base for the crannog. Just beneath the water level there would have been a secret causeway to allow the inhabitants to cross to and from land.

Many objects from Celtic times have been found near Loch Tay and archaeologists and historians believe that there were once as many as 18 crannogs on Loch Tay. Recently some archaeologists have built their own crannog on the loch as part of their investigations into the early inhabitants of Scotland.

Source A

A modern reconstruction of a crannog built on Loch Tay. ▲

The Scotii tribe

Dunadd is situated in Argyll, near to Loch Fyne. Here there is a flat rock with the shape of a footprint worn out of the rock. The early Celtic kings were crowned here. It was believed that only a man whose foot fitted the imprint on the rock could become king. Dunadd was the centre of power of the Scotii, a Celtic tribe from Ireland, who migrated to Scotland in the fourth and fifth centuries AD. The Scotii are important because they gave Scotland its name. Irish migration to the west of Scotland means that the Gaelic still spoken in parts of Scotland and Ireland are very similar.

The migration of the Scotii also led to the coming of Christianity to Scotland. Saint Columba travelled from Ireland and established a monastery on the Island of Iona off the west coast of Scotland. From this base Columba and his followers converted most of Scotland and the North of England to Christianity. The Christianity of the early Celtic Church was different from that of the established church based in Rome.

Questions

1. In which parts of Scotland did the Celts build brochs?

2. List the advantages and disadvantages of living in a broch.

3. In what ways was a dun different from a broch?

4. Describe a crannog.

5. Why did crannogs have a secret causeway?

6. Why is Dunadd important?

7. Where did the Scotii come from? In what way are the Scotii still remembered?

8. Why was Saint Columba important to the development of religious life in Britain?

Source B

The Romans ... were terrified by the fine order of the Celtic host, and the dreadful din, for there were innumerable horn-blowers and trumpeters and the whole army were shouting their war cries.

Polybius, second century BC Greek historian.

Source A

The whole race ... is madly fond of war, high-spirited and quick to battle ... on whatever excuse you stir them up, you will have them ready to face danger, even if they have nothing on their side but their own strength and courage.

Strabo, first century BC Greek geographer and historian.

— Warriors in battle

In Source A Strabo is describing how the Celtic warriors seemed to enjoy fighting and were very brave going into battle. Several Roman sources describe tall, muscular warriors who were difficult opponents. The bravery of the Celts may have been due to the belief promoted by the Druids that the soul of a warrior does not die in battle but passes on to another body. The Celtic warriors also wore torcs (a kind of necklace), which they believed gave them magical protection in battle.

According to Roman sources the Celts prepared for battle by painting their bodies using woad (a blue dye). They believed that this gave them added protection. Before going into battle the Celts performed war dances accompanied by war cries and blaring trumpets. The noise created by the Celts and their trumpets must have been a terrifying sound for opponents. In Source B, Polybius describes the scene before a battle in the second century BC.

— Weaponry

The Celtic warriors had iron swords, which were used for cutting and slashing. They also had daggers for close-range fighting and spears or javelins to throw at the enemy. The handles of their swords and daggers were finely decorated. They carried a long shield, made from wood and leather, which protected most of their body.

— Chariots

Some Celtic warriors rode into battle in light two-wheeled chariots. The chariot was drawn by two horses, and could carry a driver and a warrior. In battle the driver controlled the chariot, while the warrior could throw javelins at opponents.

Celtic warriors with their weaponry. ▶

The Celtic chariots gave the Romans some serious problems. It took them some time to find a way of dealing with the devastating effect the chariot had. When Julius Caesar fought the Celts in Britain he was impressed by the use of the chariot in battle by the Celts (see Source C).

Until a few years ago there was very little evidence to give us an idea of what chariots looked like. Recently, well-preserved items have been dredged from a lake in La Tene, Switzerland and there have been a number of discoveries in Yorkshire.

Source C

In chariot fighting the Britons begin by driving all over the field hurling javelins, and generally the terror inspired by the horses and the noise of the wheels are sufficient to throw their opponents' ranks into disorder. Then, after making their way between the squadrons of their own cavalry, they jump down from the chariots and fight on foot. In the meantime their charioteers move a short distance away from the battle and place the chariots so that their masters have an easy means of retreat to their own lines. Thus they combine the mobility of cavalry with the staying power of infantry; and by daily training and practice they gain such skill that even on a steep hill they are able to control the horses at full gallop, and to check and turn them in a moment.

*Julius Caesar, **Gallic Wars**, describing the Celts in battle.*

Raiding

Raiding was a popular and essential part of the life of Celtic warriors. Through raids young men could show their bravery and courage and gain status within the tribe. It was also important training for war, allowing the warriors to practise their horsemanship and their use of weapons. Raids also brought rewards: plunder, precious goods, prisoners who would become slaves … and heads! Returning home from a successful raid or battle the Celtic warrior would proudly display as trophies the heads of his defeated enemies.

Questions

1. According to Strabo (Source A), what were Celtic warriors like?

2. How did each of the following contribute to the bravery of Celtic warriors?

   > Druids   Torcs   Woad

3. Describe the ways in which Celtic warriors prepared for battle.

4. Describe how the Celts used their weapons in battle.

5. Read Caesar's account of the Celtic use of chariots. Select evidence or phrases from his account to support the statement 'Caesar was impressed by the Celtic use of chariots in battle'.

6. Why were many young Celtic men keen to go on raids?

7. What were the favourite trophies of Celtic warriors?

Extended writing

1. What evidence supports the view that the Romans feared and respected the Celts as fighters and opponents?

Like the Ancient Egyptians, the Celts took a great pride in their appearance. Many Celtic mirrors have been discovered providing evidence of their concern about how they looked. It also illustrates the skill of Celtic craftsmen who made bronze mirrors with intricate designs.

Celtic art

The Celts loved beautiful objects and so the work of Celtic artists was in great demand. Owning fine objects was a sign of a person's wealth and power. The richest and most beautiful objects made by Celtic artists would be for the wealthy chiefs and their families.

Celtic artists used their skills to make a variety of objects. Everyday objects such as harnesses, mirrors and coins were beautifully decorated with designs in bronze and enamel. The Celts were very fond of jewellery and many examples have survived of the fine work of Celtic artists and craftsmen.

Source A

An enamelled bronze brooch and a gold torc.

Source B

Celtic craftsmen made weapons and tools from iron but they used bronze to add decoration to the hilts of swords and daggers. **Scabbards** (sheaths for weapons) and shields were also finely decorated. Celtic artists in Britain and Ireland had special techniques that used circles and compasses to illustrate their work. They also worked the faces of animals and people into their designs.

The Celts had a passion for horses, which they used in raids and battles. The Celts expressed their love of horses through their crafts and art. For their chariots, and for the horses' harnesses, their smiths made intricate metal fittings. Horses also appear on many of their coins.

Celtic language

The early Celts spoke various languages and dialects but they did not have a written language. The Druids and bards passed on history and traditions to new generations. In Britain and Ireland a form of writing in stone was developed: this was called **Ogham**. Tall, carved stones can be seen in many parts of Scotland and Ireland with inscriptions on the stones describing important events, battles or praising heroes or chieftains. Archaeologists think that some of these stones were dedicated to Celtic gods.

The early Christian missionaries adapted the style of stone carvings to promote the new religion. They hoped to show that the Christian god was more powerful than the Celtic gods. The Picts, who were descended from the Celts, carried on the tradition of carving stones. Later the Celtic standing stones were converted into Celtic Crosses, such as Saint Martin's Cross in Iona, built around AD 700.

St Martin's Cross, Iona. ▶

The Book of Kells

Roman conquest and influence and the coming of Christianity led to the decline of the power of the Celts. However, in the area of Celtic art, Christianity brought a revival, which some historians have described as a 'golden age'. The Book of Kells, the greatest example of Celtic art, emerged from this period (around AD800) when the Celts began to embrace Christianity.

◀ *An illustration from the Book of Kells.*

The Book of Kells is an illustrated manuscript containing the Gospels of Matthew, Mark, Luke and John. It combines Celtic art and Christian belief. It was beautifully decorated by Celtic monks.

The Book of Kells is kept in Trinity College, Dublin, and a different page is displayed every day. It is a major tourist attraction and evidence of the achievements of the Celts and the beauty of Celtic art.

Every brooch, every armlet, every bracelet, every ornamentation of a sword, every movement upon the clay of a pot, every curl, curve and curlicue ever contemplated, attempted, completed by a Celtic artist – once the Celtic civilisation had come into its own – may be perceived in the Book of Kells.

Frank Delaney, **The Celts,** *describing the Book of Kells.*

41

Questions

1. How do we know that the Celts took a great pride in their appearance?

2. What types of objects and jewellery were made by Celtic craftsmen?

3. In what ways do the art and crafts of the Celts show their love of horses?

4. What uses were made of Ogham?

5. What is the connection between Standing Stones and Celtic Crosses?

6. Where is the Book of Kells and what does it contain?

Extended writing

1. Why is the Book of Kells important for studying the Celts?

c. 753 BC	**The beginning of Rome.** Villages are built on seven hills near the River Tiber in Italy and grow until they merge to form the city of Rome.
c. 510 BC	**The last king of Rome.** Rome becomes a **republic** when the citizens of Rome drive out their last king, Tarquin the Proud (in a republic the people choose their leaders).
400 BC	**Rome attacked.** The Celts sack Rome but quickly withdraw.
300 BC–220 BC	**A period of conquest.** By 250 BC the Roman republic grows as the Roman army conquers its neighbours until Rome dominates all of Italy. The Romans win the First Punic War against Carthage, in what is modern Tunisia.
202 BC–218 BC	**Wars with neighbouring powers.** Rome emerges victorious in wars with Greece and Carthage. In the Second Punic War, Hannibal, the Carthaginian general, defeats the Romans in several battles but fails to capture Rome itself. Eventually the power of Rome proves too much and Carthage is defeated.
c. 150 BC	**Expansion.** Carthage is conquered and the Romans begin the conquest of southern Gaul (modern France).
55 BC	**Invasion of Britain.** Having taken over large areas of Gaul the Roman general Julius Caesar leads the first Roman invasion of Britain in 55 BC, trying again in 54 BC to conquer Britain.
44 BC	**The assassination of Julius Caesar.** There is a period of civil wars when Rome's leaders fight among themselves. These wars end when Julius Caesar becomes **dictator** (a supreme ruler supported by the army). However, Julius Caesar is in turn assassinated in 44 BC.
27 BC	**The birth of the Roman Empire.** The first Roman Emperor, Augustus, defeats Mark Antony in a battle for the leadership of Rome, ending the period of civil wars and establishing the Roman Empire with himself as emperor.
C. AD 1	**The birth of Jesus Christ.** Jesus is born in Palestine, which at the time is a province of the Roman Empire. Jesus is crucified by the Romans in AD 33 when Pontius Pilate is the Roman governor.
AD 43	**The second invasion of Britain.** Claudius becomes emperor and begins the conquest of Britain.
AD 122	**Hadrian's Wall built.** Emperor Hadrian orders the building of this wall to protect the Roman areas of Britain from attack by tribes from Scotland.
AD 200–312	**Roman Empire under threat.** Barbarians attack the outer **provinces** (areas) of the empire. Within the empire Christians are persecuted until in AD 312 Emperor Constantine became a Christian.
AD 337	**The Roman Empire divides.** After the death of Constantine the Roman Empire is too large to defend properly. It is split in two: the eastern part, called Byzantium is ruled from Constantinople (today known as Istanbul).
AD 410	**The fall of the Roman Empire.** The Romans no longer control Britain. The Roman Empire collapses under attacks from barbarian tribes from the north and east. Rome is sacked by the Visigoths.

The Roman Empire covered the period from before the birth of Christ until over 400 years after the birth of Christ. In the West the way of counting years and dates is based on Christianity and the birth of Jesus Christ. Therefore all dates before the birth of Christ are referred to by historians as BC (Before Christ). Note that the further back in time you go before the birth of Christ the bigger the number. All dates after the birth of Christ are known as AD, which means Anno Domini which is Latin for 'in the year of Our Lord'.

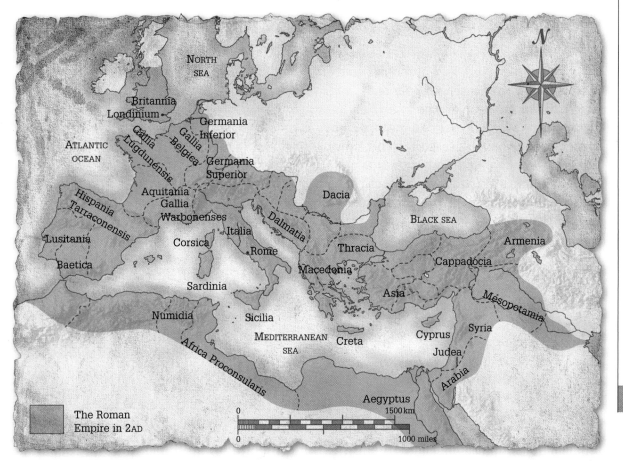

The extent of the Roman Empire in Europe and North Africa. ▲

Questions

1. Using an atlas and the map above, identify as many modern countries as you can that would have been part of the Roman Empire.

2. Put the following events in chronological order.

The assassination of Julius Caesar	The creation of the Roman Empire
Roman victory in the Punic Wars	The founding of Rome
The birth of Jesus Christ	The first Roman Invasion of Britain
The Roman conquest of Britain	The building of Hadrian's Wall

3. Explain the terms BC and AD.

Extension task

1. Draw a timeline of the history of Ancient Rome including the following periods:

The growth of Rome	Britain as part of Roman Empire
Republic and expansion	Roman Empire under threat
Establishment of the Roman Empire	Decline of the Roman Empire

The first invasion

In 55 BC, the Roman general Julius Caesar was fighting the Gauls. When Caesar heard that the Gauls were receiving help and supplies from the people living in a neighbouring island he decided that they should be punished. He sailed with his army across the Channel from France to Britain. Anxious Britons watched the approaching fleet from the cliff tops to see what would happen (see Source A).

After winning a few battles against the British tribes in southeast England, Caesar and his army went back to Gaul. The next summer, he returned and there was more fighting. This second campaign was more successful and some defeated tribes agreed to send tributes (payments) regularly to Rome. Pleased with this, Caesar left. Although the Romans found that Britain had tin and iron they did not think they could exploit these resources. Source B gives some clues to Roman motives in invading Britain.

Julius Caesar was the first Roman general to come to Britain but he did not conquer the Britons, nor did the Romans settle in Britain. In fact, they did not return for nearly 100 years, although contacts between Rome and Britain continued.

Caesar kept a diary during his campaigns in Britain. From it, historians have been able to find out a lot about what the Britons were like and how they lived and fought.

The conquest of Britain

As the emperor, Claudius was commander-in-chief of the army – but he was not a soldier. To win the respect of his legions he needed to lead them to victory. He decided that a successful invasion of Britain would keep his soldiers loyal.

In AD 43, about 40,000 soldiers sailed to Britain and landed near Richborough in Kent. The British tribes fought bravely but were no match for the Romans.

Source A

Our men hesitated, mainly because of the deep water. At this critical moment the standard-bearer of the Tenth Legion, after calling on the gods to bless the legion through his act, shouted, 'Come on, men! Jump, unless you want to betray your standard to the enemy! I, at any rate, shall do my duty to my country and my commander'.

He threw himself into the sea and started forward with the eagle. The rest were not going to disgrace themselves; cheering wildly they leaped down, and when the men in the next ships saw them, they too quickly follow their example.

Evidence of this event is based on Caesar's own account in his **Gallic Wars.**

Source B

We await news of the war in Britain ... it has become clear that there is not a scrap of silver on the island; there is no prospect of booty except slaves.

A letter from Cicero, a Roman politician, 54 BC.

Source C

The most civilised of the Britons are those who live in Kent. Tin is found in the midland area, and iron near the coast, but not in large quantities.

Julius Caesar, **Gallic Wars,** *52 BC.*

Source D

Britain produces corn, cattle, gold, silver and iron ... but there would be no advantage in taking over and holding the country as the cost of keeping a force in Britain would be greater than the revenue raised.

Strabo, Greek Geographer, AD 20.

The Romans fought their way inland and marched towards Colchester, the centre of the Catuvellauni tribe.

Aulus Platius, a Roman general, sent for Claudius. He arrived in time to lead his army into Colchester, where eleven British kings surrendered to him. He then returned to Italy, leaving his **legions** (see page 46) to conquer the rest of Britain.

Not all the British tribes surrendered and many continued to fight so the Romans attacked tribal settlements and laid siege to hill-forts. Only the tribes in Scotland were able to defy the Romans, and Scotland never became part of the Roman Empire.

Roman Britain. ▼

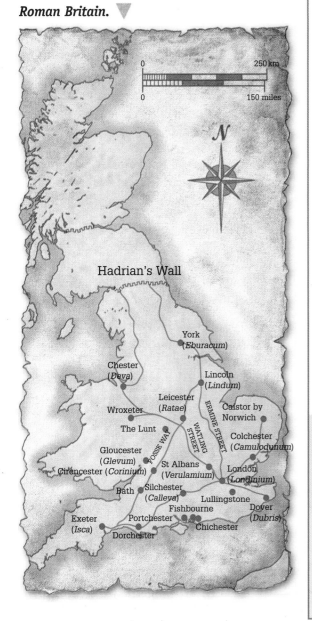

Questions

1. Using Source A, show how the action of the standard-bearer of the Tenth Legion helped in the first Roman invasion of Britain.

2. Describe the Roman invasion of Britain in AD 43.

3. Compare Sources A, B and C as evidence. Which do you think is the most reliable, and why?

4. In the first invasion of Britain, what were the aims of the Romans?

5. Why did Emperor Claudius order the conquest of Britain?

6. Who was the Roman general who led the attack on Britain in AD 43?

7. In which town did the majority of British tribes surrender to the Romans?

8. Which part of mainland Britain was not successfully conquered by the Romans?

Extended writing

1. Describe the first Roman invasion of Britain. You should mention the standard-bearer, Julius Caesar, the reasons for the invasion, when it took place, and how successful it was.

2. Explain why it took so long for the Romans to conquer Britain after the first invasions in the time of Julius Caesar.

The organisation of the Roman army.

With their well-organised and highly trained army, the Roman leaders were able to conquer many countries, and the empire spread quickly. The army was divided into **legions** of foot soldiers. Each legion was commanded by a veteran general, or *legatus*, with six tribunes – who were usually young aristocrats – as officers. A legion usually was made up of 10 **cohorts** of about 500 men each. The first cohort was special, as it was made up of twice as many men as the others. Cohorts were divided into six **centuries**, having 80 men who were under the command of a junior officer, a **centurion**. A centurion wore silvered mail and leg armour called greaves, and he fought with a sword only. His chest amulet and belt showed his rank. The legion's smallest unit was the **contubernia**, a squad of about eight men.

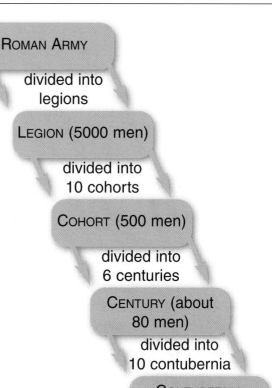

ROMAN ARMY

divided into legions

LEGION (5000 men)

divided into 10 cohorts

COHORT (500 men)

divided into 6 centuries

CENTURY (about 80 men)

divided into 10 contubernia

CONTUBERNIA (about 8 men)

46

Roman soldiers

The Roman soldiers were skilled in fighting pitched battles and in laying siege to enemy camps. They took great pride in their skills and in their victories. Each legion had an Eagle standard carried into battle by a standard-bearer. To lose a battle or to lose their standard would be considered a disgrace.

Source A

If soldiers desert their posts ... the tribune calls the legion on parade ... he chooses by lot ... about a tenth of those who have shown themselves guilty of cowardice. Those on whom the lot has fallen are clubbed to death.

Polybius, in his book **The Rise of the Roman Empire,** *written around 110 BC, explains how discipline was maintained.*

Legionaries

The well-disciplined and highly organised force of professional soldiers called legionaries maintained the supremacy of Rome. The Roman army also acted as policemen in the various provinces of the empire. A recruit enlisted for 25 years and after a period of tough training joined one of 28 legions that formed the backbone of the Roman army. A typical legionary wore a sleeveless coat of iron mail over a woollen tunic. An iron helmet protected the soldier's head and face, and a large wooden shield covered with leather and bound with iron protected most of his body. Strong leather sandals allowed him to keep up a steady marching pace. On the march legionaries carried all the tools and equipment needed for building roads and camps. His most formidable weapon was the **pilum**, a weighted throwing spear with a point sharp enough to pierce armour, but in close combat he used a short sword, or **gladius**.

To defend themselves in battle, legionary soldiers grouped together and made a shell-like defence with their shields. It was called a 'tortoise'. This ability to act as a unit helped the Roman army to many victories against fierce but less disciplined enemies.

We have ... mighty shields, with which we keep our entire bodies protected, two-edged swords, and instead of a spear, the javelin, a missile that cannot be dodged.

The Roman writer Dionysius described the successful use of these weapons in Roman Antiquities written in 30 BC.

Roman legionary soldiers in a 'tortoise' formation.

Source B

Auxiliary soldiers

The legions were supported by units of auxiliary soldiers, with about 500 men in each unit. These soldiers were often specialist fighters, such as archers, slingers and cavalrymen. Unlike legionary soldiers, auxiliary troops were not Roman citizens. They were recruited from countries the Romans had conquered.

47

Pitching camp

When the Roman soldiers were on the march they had to pitch camp every night. They dug a deep ditch all around the campsite and placed wooden stakes along the inside edge of the ditch to make a wall. This gave some protection in case they were attacked. Some soldiers dug toilets and rubbish pits; others collected water and firewood for cooking the evening meal. Their leather tents were big enough for eight men to sleep in.

Questions

1. Describe how the Roman army was organised.

2. What was a contubernia?

3. Explain the position of each of the following:

   legatus   centurion   standard-bearer

4. Describe the weapons and armour of a legionary. What else would the Roman legionaries carry on their marches?

5. Describe the tactics used by the Roman army in battle.

6. In what ways were the auxiliary soldiers different from the legionaries?

7. Besides fighting what other jobs might Roman soldiers have?

Extended writing

1. How was discipline maintained in the Roman army?

2. What part did the Roman army play in building and controlling the Roman Empire?

Resistance to the Romans

── Caractacus, the first British hero

Caractacus was the king of the Catuvellauni at the time of the second Roman invasion. Caractacus and his brother, Togodumnus, became the leaders of an anti-Roman campaign that managed to resist the invaders for nearly nine years.

After some early defeats in the east of Britain, Caractacus moved west into lands that would be easier to defend. His small army survived a battle with the Romans in the land of the Silures (modern-day Glamorgan, in Wales) and Caractacus moved north to find the ideal location for a final, decisive battle.

Caractacus was finally defeated by the Roman governor Ostorious Scapula, in AD 51, but Caractacus was not killed in the battle and managed to escape to the land of the Brigantes in northern Britain, where he hoped to find safety. However, Cartimandua, the Queen of the Brigantes, handed Caractacus over to the Romans.

He was sent to Rome along with other captives, where he came to Emperor Claudius' attention for his courtesy and was pardoned. He and his family were allowed to live out their lives in peace in Italy.

── *What do we know about Boudica?*

Boudica, whose name in the language of the Iceni means 'victory', was the queen of the Iceni tribe, based in Norfolk; her husband was Prasutagus. During his reign Prasutagus had become wealthy and had become friendly with the Romans. When he died he left everything to his two daughters and the Emperor Nero, in equal shares, thinking that this would provide peace for his kingdom and his family.

However, when the Roman soldiers came to meet Boudica they did not treat her as a queen but as an ordinary subject of Nero. Boudica was flogged and her daughters were assaulted. The Roman tax collector in London, Catus Decianus, expected them to pay their taxes like all Roman subjects. Boudica's revenge was fierce and bloody.

Source B

▲ *A nineteenth-century statue of Boudica on the Embankment in London.*

Source A

Of the largest size, most terrible of aspect, most savage of countenance and harsh of voice; having a profusion of red hair which fell down to her hips, and wearing a great collar of gold. She had on a floating robe of many colours, drawn close about her, and over this she wore a thick mantle fastened by a clasp. Such was her usual dress; but at this time she also bore a spear.

Tacitus, a Roman historian, describing Boudica.

Case Study – Boudica's revolt

Boudica, with 120,000 tribesmen under her command, attacked Colchester and totally destroyed the town and its Roman garrison. News of the rebellion reached Lincoln and the Roman Ninth Legion marched towards Colchester: they were ambushed and wiped out in what was Boudica's greatest victory and one of Rome's worst defeats.

Boudica's next target was London. She burned London, killing 70,000 people.

Source C

Victims were impaled on stakes to the accompaniment of sacrifices, feasting and orgies.

Evidence of Boudica's treatment of London and its population is based on accounts of the Greek historian, Cassius Dio.

After London Boudica's warriors ransacked the Roman town of Verulamium (now known as St Albans). Only one Roman force stood between Boudica and total victory against the Romans: the army of Suetonius Paulinus.

Until this point the rebellion had succeeded through fury, surprise and luck. However, in the next battle the advantages lay with the disciplined and well-organised Roman force. British fighting tactics had changed little since the days of Caesar's invasions: cavalry and infantry were mixed up, chariots were still used, and women and children came along as spectators to watch the fight. Before the battle Boudica tried to encourage her army to fight to the death for their freedom.

Many Britons died and the Romans won a crushing victory. Details of the length of the battle are uncertain, but 400 Romans and 80,000 Britons were killed.

How Boudica died cannot be certain: no Britons survived the slaughter to tell her tale. Boudica's rebellion was defeated and Britain remained a Roman colony for nearly 400 years.

49

Questions

1. In your exercise book write the heading: 'The revolt of Caractacus'. Then re-arrange the following events into chronological order:

Caractacus was defeated by the Romans in AD 51
Defeated in the east Caractacus fled to Wales in the west
Caractacus was handed over to the Romans
Caractacus was pardoned by Emperor Claudius
Caractacus was taken to Rome in chains
Claudius ordered the conquest of Britain in AD 43
Caractacus and his brother began the revolt against the Romans

2. Why could Emperor Claudius be regarded as merciful?

3. In pairs discuss the following aspects of Boudica's revolt:

The reasons for the revolt
Boudica's treatment of the enemy
Boudica's leadership
Why she finally lost

4. Write a report on 'The failure of Boudica's revolt'. In your report you should refer to: the reasons why Boudica revolted against the Romans, Boudica's successes in the campaign, the reasons why the revolt eventually failed.

— *Roman forts*

Whenever the Roman army conquered an area of Britain they built a fort to protect themselves and the land they had gained. The typical Roman fort had a garrison of up to 500 men. Building the fort was carried out by the Roman legionaries, helped by the auxiliary troops. The forts were built to a standard plan: there were major Roman forts at Caerleon, Chester and York. The unfinished Roman fort at Inchtuthil in Perthshire in Scotland was built to the same plan as Caerleon.

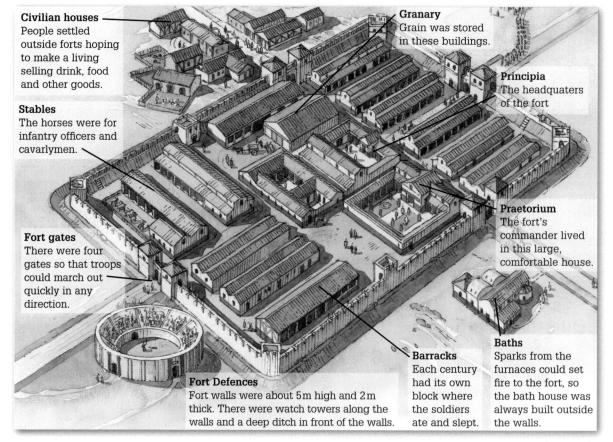

Civilian houses
People settled outside forts hoping to make a living selling drink, food and other goods.

Stables
The horses were for infantry officers and cavarlymen.

Fort gates
There were four gates so that troops could march out quickly in any direction.

Granary
Grain was stored in these buildings.

Principia
The headquaters of the fort

Praetorium
The fort's commander lived in this large, comfortable house.

Fort Defences
Fort walls were about 5m high and 2m thick. There were watch towers along the walls and a deep ditch in front of the walls.

Barracks
Each century had its own block where the soldiers ate and slept.

Baths
Sparks from the furnaces could set fire to the fort, so the bath house was always built outside the walls.

A plan of a Roman fort. ▲

The standard shape of a fort was oblong, with rounded corners. The major forts, like Chesters fort near Hadrian's Wall, were surrounded by an outer wall about two metres thick with a double ditch outside and an earth **rampart** inside (a rampart is a platform which allows soldiers inside to see over the wall). The outer wall was patrolled by sentries, who also guarded each gate. The main buildings in the centre were the headquarters of the fort and the general's quarters. Within the fort there were also granaries, workshops, a hospital and the barracks. Outside the main forts were **amphitheatres** (a circle or half-circle of seats around a central area) for training and entertainment, and a bathhouse. Traders were attracted by the forts and set up shop close by leading to the growth of towns.

Case Study – Hadrian's Wall

Emperor Hadrian ordered the army to build this wall in AD 122. It took six years for the Roman legionaries to build and was 80 Roman miles long (117 km or 73 modern miles), from Wallsend-on-Tyne in the east to Bowness-on-Solway in the west, almost the same as the modern border between Scotland and England (see the map on page 45).

There are many theories about why the wall was built but it is generally agreed that Hadrian wanted to mark the northern boundary of his empire. Expansion further north came later when from AD 140 – 163 Hadrian's Wall was briefly replaced by the Antonine Wall. (See also the section 'The Romans In Scotland'.)

The wall was very cleverly built and Emperor Hadrian praised the Roman soldiers for their efficiency as engineers. The site of the wall was chosen to make the best use of natural defences. Every Roman mile there was a **milecastle** guarded by at least eight men.

At regular intervals between milecastles were turrets where sentries kept watch so they could check the movement of goods, people and animals along the frontier. During the building of the wall, large forts were built along it and these served as crossing points, for example, Housesteads and Castlesteads. Civilian settlements grew up around these forts.

To the north of the wall was a deep defensive ditch and to the south another ditch, the vallum, flanked by mounds of earth. The vallum was the Roman equivalent of a barbed-wire fence.

By the early AD 400s, the empire was in decline and Britain became cut off from Rome. Frontier defences were neglected and as pay ceased to arrive, soldiers drifted away. Gradually, the wall's stones reappeared in local farmhouses, field walls and even churches. It was only relatively recently that interest in the wall as an archaeological monument, and as a place to visit, grew.

51

Questions

1. Copy and complete the following table:

Why were forts built?	Who built the forts?	List three forts in Roman Britain

2. Draw a plan of a typical Roman fort. Include in your plan all the main features listed right and describe what they were used for.

barracks	granaries	ramparts
ditch	workshops	hospital

3. How did Hadrian's Wall get its name?

4. Where and when was Hadrian's Wall built?

Extended writing

1. Working with a partner, decide why the Romans chose this particular part of Britain to build a wall. You should refer to the text, map and an atlas.

2. Why is Hadrian's Wall a useful piece of evidence for historians today?

22 Roman roads

One of the greatest and long-lasting of the things the Romans brought to Britain was the road system. The roads that the Romans built were designed mainly for the army. Roman troops could march more than 50 kilometres a day – if the roads were firm and dry.

Building roads

In damp climates, road building was a complex task. The roadbed had to be **cambered** (curved outwards) so water would run off into the ditches at the sides. To provide a firm cushion for heavy loads, the foundation was made up of compact layers. In most cases, sand was deposited at the bottom of the road and rolled flat. Small stones and pebbles made up the second layer, gravel the third, and paving stones were then laid on top. This hard-wearing surface carried troops and supply wagons, merchant's carts and postal carriages.

Cambered surface

Gravel

Stones

Pebbles

Sand

Roadside ditches

A cross-section diagram of a Roman road. ▲

Road building was a hard task and required a disciplined work force. Roman soldiers did most of the work, which kept them fit and busy between campaigns, although on rare occasions the soldiers rebelled. Sometimes the Romans forced people they had conquered, such as the Caledonians of Britain, to work in building the roads.

— *The road network*

In Roman Britain towns were linked together by a complex network of major and minor roads. London had become the most important seaport of Roman Britain and was at the heart of the road network. Three important Roman roads in Britain were **Ermine Street**, which ran from London to York, and beyond that to Corbridge near Hadrian's Wall (today the A1 follows approximately the same route); **Watling Street**, which linked London with the important Roman town of Chester to the northwest; and **Fosse Way**, which allowed the rapid movement of men and materials from Lincoln to Exeter and the southwest. (See the map on page 45.)

Roman roads were built with great skill and ran in as straight a line as possible, much like modern motorways. This meant that troops, supplies and trade could travel as quickly as possible. In Britain the Roman roads united the country in a network of communications. The distances were marked by Roman milestones. Roman officials and soldiers moved along them to control and govern the land.

The roads were also a vital communications link as they carried the **Imperial Post**: this was used to send instructions from the government in Rome to the provinces of the empire. There were posting stations at regular intervals – usually about 24 kilometres – along the roads, where travellers could rest for the night and get a change of horses.

53

Questions

1. Show how the Romans could be considered good engineers.

2. Who usually did the actual hard work of building the roads?

3. Match the following Roman roads to their destinations:

Name of road	Destination
Ermine Street	London to
Watling Street	London to
Fosse Way	Exeter to

4. What type of traffic used the Roman roads in Britain?

Extended writing

1. The Roman roads linked the main Roman towns such as London and Chester. 'Chester' was a Roman term used for a settlement and many Roman towns have names that end in -chester. Working in pairs, use an atlas and find as many towns as you can in England which end in -chester.

2. What were the benefits to the Romans of having such good roads?

3. Imagine you travelled from London to Chester in Roman times. Write a detailed description of your journey: include who and what you saw, how you travelled, where you stayed etc.

23 Daily life in Roman Britain

Before the Roman conquest, Britons lived on farms or in hill-forts built for defence and security. To the Britons towns were a new Roman idea; to the Romans towns were a mark of **civilisation**. Wherever the Romans conquered lands they encouraged the building of towns.

Roman towns

Most Roman towns were built to a similar pattern. Finding a clean and regular water supply was the first stage, and then the roads were laid out, crossing each other at right angles. All the main buildings were inside a wall, with a ditch as additional protection. The main buildings in a Roman town, such as Bath, Chester or Silchester, were the temples, bathhouses and the town hall, or Basilica as it was known to the Romans, where people paid their taxes. Near the Basilica was a large, open area surrounded by shops and offices known as the **Forum**: this would be the busiest part of a Roman town.

Source A

The Forum in Rome.

In Rome itself the Forum was the most important part of the city. It was here that the politicians met to make decisions, where court cases were held and where traders sold their goods. It was usually in the Forum that the largest temples were built and here that the main religious ceremonies and festivals were held.

Villas

Roman landowners in Britain lived in luxurious buildings known as villas. The villas were made of brick with red tile roofs, with rooms and balconies arranged around a central courtyard. These villas would be well decorated with wall paintings and mosaic floors and some even had central heating which was provided by **hypocausts**, a system of underfloor heating.

The Romans enjoyed eating. The main meal of the day was eaten in the evening. While the women and children ate separately, the men would recline on settees around a low table in the dining room (*triclinium*) and be served by slaves. They enjoyed many different foods from all areas of the empire, using their fingers to eat rather than forks. To accompany the food the Romans liked to drink wine.

Childhood in Roman times

Children wore a special locket around their neck, given to them at birth, called a bulla. It contained an amulet as a protection against evil. Girls wore their bulla until they were married when the bulla was put aside with other things like toys. Boys wore the bulla until the day they became a citizen around their sixteenth or seventeenth birthday.

The children of Roman citizens attended school, starting very early in the morning, where they learned reading, writing and counting with Roman numerals. As the boys grew older they studied Latin, Greek, grammar and literature and some went on to study public speaking, which was seen as very important. The children of the poor were unlikely to go to school but may have been taught some basics at home by their parents.

Roman religion

Worshipping their gods was part of everyday life for the Romans. They believed in more than one god. In fact they had a god for every area of their daily life. They also adopted local gods from different parts of the empire; for example they believed in the Persian god Mithras. Sometimes they even made their emperors, living and dead, into gods.

The Romans believed that if they worshipped the gods and made offerings to them then the gods would protect them in their everyday lives. They also believed that it was very important to make special offerings to gods like Saturn, the God of Farming, who could help crops to grow. Soldiers believed that the gods would help and protect them in battle. Roman soldiers would pray to Mars, the God of War. Archaeologists have uncovered evidence of Roman worship in Britain: there were temples and statues in honour of Mithras in London and other Roman towns. In Scotland too the Roman soldiers left behind evidence of their worship of different gods, for example the dedication to Jupiter, King of the Gods, at Carriden in West Lothian.

55

Questions

1. Name three Roman towns in Britain.

2. Describe the layout of a typical Roman town.

3. Explain why

   a. the Basilica may have been an unpopular place.
   b. the Forum was a popular and important place.

4. Working in pairs, copy and complete the table below.

Roman times	Today
Homes	
Food	
Children's clothes	
School	

Extended writing

1. Using the information in the table, and referring back to previous chapters, write a report highlighting the main similarities and differences between life in the time of the Romans and life today.

Source B

The Roman god Jupiter. ▲

In Rome the public baths were extremely popular. Roman men and women tried to visit the baths at least once every day. The baths had hot and cold pools, towels, slaves to wait on you, steam rooms, saunas and exercise rooms. At one time, there were as many as 900 public baths in Ancient Rome. Small ones held about 300 people, and the big ones held 1500 people or more. In all but the largest baths, there were separate hours for men and women – the women's time slot was much shorter.

Why were Roman baths so popular?

The bathhouse was not just a place where Romans went to keep clean. It was also a meeting place. The Roman baths consisted of a series of rooms. The floors were covered in mosaics with walls made of veined marble. The main rooms were:

- *The frigidarium* – a very cold room.
- *The tepidarium* – a warm room.
- *The caldarium* – a hot room.
- *The laconicum* – a very hot room.

The Romans introduced bathing to Britain and baths became a feature of all the main Roman towns in Britain. Some wealthy people had baths built into their houses but most people went along to the public baths. There they met friends while sitting in hot rooms, having massages and swimming in the large baths.

Roman baths not only encouraged cleanliness but were also important social centres where citizens could meet, exercise or relax and gossip. The Romans did not have soap so **strigils** were used to scrape off body dirt and sweat. Then bath attendants would massage the bathers with sweet-smelling oils or perfumes.

Roman baths in Britain

The most famous Roman baths in Britain are in Bath, in England (called Aquae Sulis by the Romans). Here there is a temple to Sulis Minerva. She was the goddess associated with the warm-water spring that bubbled into the main bath. This warm water was thought to have healing powers. The remains of a Roman bathhouse can be seen at Bearsden near Glasgow.

The walls of a Roman bathhouse were very thick to conserve the heat, which came from furnaces sending warm air into the area below the floor. This was known as a hypocaust and provided Roman baths and the homes of richer Romans with a form of central heating.

Source A

Roman baths in Bath, England. ▲

57

A bathhouse needed water even more than heat. The smaller baths got their water from nearby rivers but some of the larger baths required the building of great **aqueducts** to bring water. Examples of these aqueducts have been found at Lincoln, Dorchester and Wroxeter in England.

Questions

1. What evidence is there that baths were popular in Roman times?

2. Explain the following terms:

frigidarium	tepidarium	caldarium	laconicum
strigil	hypocaust	aqueduct	Aquae Sulis

3. Why is Sulis Minerva associated with the Roman town of Bath?

4. Why did the Romans go to the baths?

5. What modern leisure centres are most like the Roman baths?

Extended writing

1. Imagine you lived in Roman Britain around AD 150. Describe a visit to a Roman bathhouse.

2. Explain how the Romans ensured that their baths

    a. had plenty of water
    b. were heated.

Roman entertainment

In the early days of the Roman Empire, violent contests between slaves were sometimes staged to mark the death of wealthy nobles. These fights gave the dead person a blood offering to the gods. These religious rituals later became part of Roman entertainment.

Case Study – Gladiators

Male slaves were sometimes bought especially to be trained as **gladiators** (professional fighters) and would fight each other in huge amphitheatres. They would even fight wild animals such as lions or bears. In gladiator schools they learned how to use different kinds of weapons for fighting. Gladiators were given special names, depending on which kind of weapon they used. The **retarius** specialised in fighting with only a net and a trident, while the **secutor** wore a helmet and used a sword.

The Colosseum in Rome was a popular venue and up to 45,000 spectators often gathered to watch bloody combat between gladiators, and battles between men and wild animals. On some occasions unarmed victims, often Christians, were sent into the arena to face hungry, wild animals. Sometimes the Romans flooded the Colosseum with water and held mock naval battles.

Soon Roman rulers learned how to exploit the popularity of these contests. Julius Caesar tried to win public support by staging a massive contest involving 640 gladiators in the arena. Great gladiatorial contests appealed to all of Roman society with **Senators** (important Roman nobles and politicians) being given special seats. However, not everyone enjoyed the contests between gladiators. The Roman writer Juvenal disapproved of this entertainment and believed that Roman citizens were only concerned with the entertainment and food provided by emperors, and were ignoring their duties as citizens.

Source A

Time was when Romans elected commanders of legions: but now ... there are only two things that concern them: bread and games.

Juvenal, AD 120.

Source B

A scene from the film **Gladiator**. ▲

Other forms of entertainment

The Romans enjoyed being entertained. In Rome the huge arenas, especially the Circus Maximus, provided venues for chariot races and even in Roman Britain chariot races were very popular. People supported their favourite chariot team the way we follow football teams and they would wear their team colours. Open-air theatres were popular in Ancient Rome and, since performances were free, they attracted large crowds to watch plays and musical performances.

The Romans also enjoyed board games with counters and dice. Hunting was also popular. People in the countryside would hunt animals for fun as well as for food.

Questions

1. Why were gladiator contests a popular form of entertainment in Roman times?

2. Describe some different types of gladiators.

3. What was Juvenal's opinion of the entertainment in the arena? Use evidence from Juvenal's description to support your answer.

Extension tasks

1. You are investigating Roman entertainment. First, decide whether the sources below are primary or secondary sources. (A primary source is written or created at the time. A secondary source is written or created many years later.) Say how useful you feel each source is.

2. Using these sources and other information in this section, write a report on the Roman attitude to entertainment. What evidence suggests that entertainment in the arena was very popular? What evidence suggests that entertainment in the arena was not popular with all Romans? Would we find this entertainment civilised?

59

Source C

One day I happened to call in at a midday show in the amphitheatre, expecting some sport, fun and relaxation. It was just the opposite. The other shows I had seen were a picnic in comparison. This was pure murder. When one man fell another took his place. And this went on and on till none was left, even the last was killed.

The Roman writer Pliny, AD 45.

Source D

Specially trained slaves called gladiators would fight each other in huge amphitheatres. When a gladiator lost a fight the emperor would ask the crowd to decide whether the gladiator should be spared to fight another day. The crowd would decide by putting their thumbs up if he should live or if they wanted the loser to die, put their thumbs down. The decision of the crowd would depend on how the gladiator had fought.

An adapted extract from The Roman Empire, written by historian John Simkin in 1991.

Source E

The wild-beast hunts, two a day for five days, were magnificent ... But what pleasure can it possibly be to a man of culture, when either a puny human being is mangled by a most powerful beast, or a splendid beast is killed with a hunting spear? The last day was the elephants and many people felt sorry for them.

From a letter by the Roman writer and politician Cicero, 55 BC.

Scotland was known to the Romans as Caledonia. In Roman times, Scotland was populated by many tribes such as the Novantae and Selgovae in southern Scotland, the Damnonii and Votadini in the midlands of Scotland, and further north the Verturiones and the Caledonii.

Roman Scotland. ▶

The invasion of Scotland

Once the Romans had conquered Roman Britain they realised that in order to protect their land they would have to go to war against the fierce tribes who lived to the north, in what is now Scotland. In AD 80 the Roman governor of Britian, Agricola, decided to conquer the Celtic and Caledonian tribes since they threatened the peace and security of Roman Britain.

Much of what we know about the Roman invasion of Scotland is based on the writings of Tacitus who was the son-in-law of Agricola. We should be careful about the evidence of writers describing someone they respect and admire as the information may be biased. However, archaeological evidence backs up many of Tacitus' descriptions.

Early campaigns

In the early campaigns the Romans conquered the tribes and lands in southern Scotland and up to the area between the Firth of Clyde and the Firth of Forth. Some of the invading Roman Legions pushed as far north as the River Tay. In a later campaign Agricola decided to deal with the tribes further north. He built a fort at Inchtuthil in Perthshire. As the Romans advanced the Celtic tribes grouped together under the leadership of Calgacus, whose Celtic name meant 'the swordsman'. The two armies clashed at a place the Romans called 'Mons Graupius'. The Roman army won the day.

Source A

Roman discipline triumphed. While the enemy were in disorder the Roman troops kept their fighting order. Agricola ordered his men to fight at close quarters. The enemy had only small shields and swords with no sharp point for thrusting. The horsemen broke the ranks of the Caledonians and rode round to take them from behind. They left 10,000 dead on the field. Bodies, arms and cut off limbs lay all around. The Romans lost only 360.

Tacitus describing the battle.

Agricola built a line of forts from Drymen in the west to Stracathro in the east but he did not manage to bring Caledonia fully under Roman control before he was summoned back to Rome by the emperor. The Romans soon abandoned these forts and retreated back to Roman Britain where they built Hadrian's Wall (see page 51) to keep the Caledonians out.

Later campaigns

Twenty years later the Romans launched a new invasion of Scotland. Having pushed northwards from Hadrian's Wall, in about AD 142 the Romans built the longest wall ever seen in Scotland, effectively cutting the country in two between the Firths of Forth and Clyde. This new wall was about 64 kilometres long, from Old Kilpatrick in the west to Boness in the east. The Romans named this wall after Emperor Antonius: it was called the Antonine Wall. The Antonine Wall had a stone base and forts along the wall; the ramparts were of turf and timber.

The Romans abandoned the Antonine Wall some years later, retreating behind Hadrian's Wall. Despite later campaigns the Romans never succeeded in conquering Scotland. However, there is a lot of evidence of their presence in Scotland. In Bearsden near Glasgow there are remains of a Roman bathhouse.

Archaeologists have uncovered Roman evidence including pottery from the fort at Cramond, nails and tools from the fort at Inchtuthil, coins in a jar found near the Antonine Wall and various stone carvings. At Carriden at the eastern end of the Antonine Wall archaeologists found a stone with the inscription:

> *This stone is dedicated to the god Jupiter by Aelius Mansuestas, who is the representative of the civilian population of Carriden.*

Questions

1. List the main tribes living in Scotland at the time of the Roman invasion.

2. What was the Roman name for Scotland?

3. Explain why Agricola decided to invade Scotland.

4. How reliable is the account of Agricola's invasion written by Tacitus?

5. Where was the Antonine Wall built? Why did the Romans choose this particular place to build the wall?

6. What evidence remains in Scotland today of the Roman presence?

Extended writing

In groups complete one of the following tasks and prepare a report on your findings which you should present to the whole class. You can use the school library or the Internet to find out more about the Romans in Scotland.

1. Why did the Romans never succeed in conquering Scotland?

2. Imagine you are a newspaper reporter. Prepare a front-page report with a headline on the Battle of Mons Graupius.

3. The Scottish Tourist Board wants to attract visitors interested in Scotland's past. Prepare a report on evidence of the Roman presence in Scotland and a list of places that tourists might visit.

The legacy of Ancient Rome

The Roman Empire fell over 1500 years ago, but the Romans left
many things behind which are still important today.

The calendar

The calendar we use today was organised by Julius Caesar in 45 BC. He changed
the start of the year from March to January and decreed that there would be 365
days in a year, with February having an extra day every fourth year: what we call
a 'leap year'. The names of the months are based on the original Latin names.

- Januarius (January) – from Janus, the two-headed god of doors, one head
  facing the old year and one the new year.
- Februarius (February) – from a Roman festival.
- Martius (March) – named after Mars, the Roman God of War.
- Aprilis (April) – from the Latin word 'to open', referring to spring.
- Maius (May) – from the goddess, Maia.
- Junius (June) – named after the goddess Juno.
- Julius (July) – named after Emperor Julius Caesar.
- Augustus (August) – named after Emperor Augustus.
- September, October, November and December were originally the seventh,
  eight, ninth and tenth months respectively and were named after the Latin
  words for seven, eight, nine and ten.

Language, literature and law

One of the most important achievements of the Romans was their literature –
books, plays and poems. In earlier sections you will have seen references to
Tacitus and other Roman writers: these books were all written in Latin. For
hundreds of years Latin was a common language used throughout western
Europe, especially by churchmen, diplomats and scholars. This language used
by the Romans still survives in written form throughout Europe. Doctors,
lawyers and scientists, for example, use many Latin phrases in their work,
such as *Homo sapiens*. Many words that we all use are based on Latin words;
for example, 'pupil' comes from the Latin *pupillum*, which means 'boy' and
'student' comes from the Latin *studium*, which means 'eager'.

Roman law, established throughout the empire, has also had an important
influence on the modern legal system in Britain and in Europe. The Romans
gave us important legal principles such as the importance of evidence, that all
citizens are equal under the law, and that the accused is entitled to a trial by a
jury and is innocent until proved guilty. Scottish law is still based on Roman law.

Architecture

The Romans developed the classical style of architecture first used in Ancient
Greece and added to it features like the arch and the dome. They built in

Source A

Arch of Constantine in Rome, built in AD316.

brick, as well as stone, and also used concrete. The Romans erected large buildings or monuments to celebrate and record their achievements, especially military victories. Examples of Roman building can still be seen today in Rome; for example the Pantheon with its wonderful dome or the remains of the Colosseum. This tradition continues today and all over the world you can see columns and arches based on the Roman style of architecture. In London, Marble Arch and Nelson's Column, both built in the nineteenth century, are built in the Roman style.

63

Source B

Marble Arch in London, built in 1829 in the style of the Arch of Constantine.

In Britain today there is considerable visible evidence of the Roman presence. It is possible to walk along sections of Hadrian's Wall and to see the remains of the many Roman forts built along the wall, like Housesteads or Newsteads. At Bath you can see an original Roman bathhouse. In Scotland, sections of the Antonine Wall can be seen and it is possible to view the remains of a Roman bathhouse at Bearsden, near Glasgow. There is also extensive archaeological evidence of the Roman presence in Britain in the form of pottery, coins, weapons, helmets and inscriptions on stone. Only recently workers building a shopping centre near Edinburgh uncovered the remains of what is believed to be a Roman chariot.

Religion

Part of the Roman legacy to Europe was Christianity. Initially the Romans were suspicious of Christianity – it was a Roman governor who had ordered Jesus to be crucified, and in the first century AD the Romans persecuted Christians. Despite this Christianity survived in the **catacombs** (underground tombs) of Rome. Emperor Constantine believed that the Christian god had helped him to victory over his enemies and he became a Christian in AD 323. Constantine encouraged others to become Christians and Christianity became the official religion of the Roman Empire, surviving the Roman Empire's fall. The Roman Catholic Church is still based in Rome today.

Extension tasks

Each group should attempt at least two of the tasks outlined below.

1. Prepare a wall display showing a calendar with the original Latin names for the months. Find out more about how the months got their names and use this information to illustrate your wall display, such as a picture of Julius Caesar or a brief account of his life to highlight the month of July.

2. Using this book and other resources (such as other textbooks, the school library, computers and the Internet) find as many Latin words and phrases as you can that are still used today. Include Latin words and phrases with their meanings in a wall display.

3. Prepare a wall display of Roman buildings and monuments.

4. Prepare a Tourist Guide for visitors interested in visible evidence of the Roman presence in Britain.